JOHN SKELTON

JOHN SKELTON

SELECTED POEMS

*edited with an introduction
by Gerald Hammond*

FYFIELD BOOKS
Carcanet   Manchester

First published in 1980 by
Carcanet New Press Ltd
330 Corn Exchange
Manchester M4 3BG

Printed in Great Britain by Billings, Guildford

CONTENTS

INTRODUCTION

No poet ever believed so strongly in his calling: *vates*, prophet, bard, maker—these are pallid when set against Skelton's pride in the word 'laureate'. 'Poet laureate', and the succession of poetasters who have filled that position, has debased the word for us, but in Skelton's self dramatisation it stands for the noblest of pursuits, defender of the king, of the faith, and of civilised values. Not only in his writings, but in every part of his life, right down to his dress, Skelton acted the part. One of his shortest Skeltonics is *Calliope*, written in answer to the question 'Why wear ye Calliope embroidered with letters of gold?' It seems that Skelton's creation as poet laureate to the University of Oxford was made before Henry VII, who had, as part of the ceremony given him a garment embroidered with 'Calliope'. That was c.1488; as with many of Skelton's poems it is not possible to give an accurate date to the poem *Calliope*, but from what it says it seems fair to ascribe it to the closing years of his life, some thirty-five years later. To the question why he wore Calliope, 'Skelton Laureate, Orator Regius, maketh this answer':

> Calliope;
> As ye may see,
> Regent is she
>   Of poets all,
> Which gave to me
> The high degree
> Laureate to be
>   Of fame royal;
> Whose name enrolled
> With silk and gold
> I dare be bold
>   Thus for to wear.
> Of her I hold
> And her household;
> Though I wax old
>   And somedele sere,
> Yet is she fain,
> Void of disdain,

> Me to retain
>> Her servitor;
> With her certain
> I will remain,
> As my sovereign
>> Most of pleasure.

And if the point is still not clear, the Latin version of the poem tells us plainly that Calliope is *Musarum excellentissima, speciosissima, formorissima, heroicis praeest versibus*; and her influence has reached into this century as Robert Graves' White Goddess.

The granting of the laureateship was one of the two great events in Skelton's life; the other was being made tutor to the future Henry VIII twelve years later. Henry was not then seen as the future king because Arthur was still alive; and soon after Arthur's death in 1502, Skelton, who had taken holy orders in 1488, was moved away from the court to the rich and comfortable living of Diss in Norfolk. He kept this living for the rest of his life, but from the time Henry became king in 1509 he involved himself in the major controversies of pre-Reformation England, the rise of humanist learning, the movement towards Lutheranism, and, above all, the power of Cardinal Wolsey. And chiefly on account of his enmity with Wolsey he lived out the last years of his life in sanctuary at Westminister.

This is where Calliope and all she stands for is important. Her inspiration gave Skelton total poetic licence to say what he wanted how he wanted. The range is impressive. He can address the most powerful and dangerous statesman in England as a source of syphilitic infection in *Why Come Ye Not To Court?*, or, more simply, as Judas Iscariot in *Speak, Parrot*. In *Colin Clout* he recovered the voice of Piers Plowman to show the English people, both laity and clergy, where their follies and vices were leading them. The clergy he saw

> With gold all betrapped
> In purple and pall belapped;
> Some hatted and some capped,
> Richly bewrapped

. . . .

> Their mules gold doth eat,
> Their neighbours die for meat.

This had led to a laity ready and eager to espouse any form of heresy, religious or political:

> And some have a smack
> Of Luther's sack,
> And a burning spark
> Of Luther's wark,
> And are somewhat suspect
> In Luther's sect;
> And some of them bark,
> Clatter and carp
> Of that heresy art
> Called Wicliffista,
> The devilish dogmatista;
> And some be Hussians,
> And some be Arians,
> And some be Pelagians,
> And make much variance
> Between the clergy
> And the temporality,
> How the Church hath too mickle,
> And they have too little..

In *The Bouge of Court* the court is peopled with hypocrites and psychopaths; in *The Tunning of Elinour Rumming* the South Eastern citizenry, from the emerging middle class down to the lowest peasantry, have no ambition more noble than to drink themselves into a stupor; and in *Magnificence*, for probably the first time in English drama, a king is shown how easily he may be corrupted by power and flattery. And always there is the voice of Skelton insisting that he has the laureate's right to say such things. He has the right, too, to tell Jane Scrope, the little girl whose lament for her dead pet he recounted in *Philip Sparrow*, that neither she nor her family should be offended by the poem's gradual revelation of his longing for her. In the 1480s, writing like a conventionally ponderous laureate poet, Skelton poured scorn on all those responsible for the death of the Earl of Northumberland:

11

Barons, knights, squires, one and all,
Together with servants of his family,
Turned their backs and let their master fall,
Of whose life they counted not a fly:
Take up whoso would, for there they let him lie.
Alas, his gold, his fee, his annual rent
Upon such a sort was ill bestowed and spent!

Forty years later his final lines of terse, bare Skeltonics proclaimed his belief in the unending war which the laureate must fight:

Therefore no grievance,
I pray you, for to take
In this that I do make
Against these frenetics,
Against these lunatics,
Against these schismatics,
Against these heretics,
Now of late abjured,
Most unhappily ured:
For be ye well assured
That frenzy, nor jealousy,
Nor heresy will never die.

And the Latin epigram to his last poem, *A Replication Against Certain Young Scholars Abjured of Late*, points forward sixty years to the Elizabethans' defences of poetry—it begins like this (in translation):

Infinite and beyond count are the sophists; infinite and beyond count are the logicians; beyond count are the philosophers, the theologians; infinite are the doctore, beyond count are the schoolmasters; but poets are few and rare—for all that is precious is rare.

In claiming and proclaiming such beliefs Skelton is at his most explicit, but this does not mean that his poetry is invariably strident or unsubtle. It sometimes is, but this is deliberate. The Skeltonic itself is ideally constructed for invective, so that in *Why Come Ye Not To Court?* the account of the anarchic evil of Wolsey is reinforced by the apparent randomness and unstoppability of the verse form; and the only way the poem can come to an end is in a piece

12

of pure name calling:

> Complain or do what ye will,
> Of your complaint it shall not skill,
> This is the tenor of my bill,
> A dawcock ye be, and so shall be still.

But the Skeltonic, too, could register the gentle tones of a quiet confidence in one's personal salvation, as in the way Colin Clout ends his poem after having travelled over the strife-ridden English countryside:

> The forecastle of my ship
> Shall glide and smoothly slip
> Out of the waves wood
> Of the stormy flood;
> Shoot anchor, and lie at road,
> And sail not far abroad,
> Till the coast be clear,
> That the lode-star appear.
> My ship now will I steer
> Toward the port salu
> Of our saviour Jesu,
> Such grace that he us send
> To rectify and amend
> Things that are amiss,
> When that his pleasure is.

Remarkable as these two poems are they do not match *Philip Sparrow*, Skelton's finest achievement in the form named after him. Here the versatility of the Skeltonic is impressive. It ranges from the Who Killed Cock Robin simplicity of Jane Scrope's recital of all the birds who will attend Philip's funeral to the barely suppressed passion of the poet as he contemplates the little girl: innocence in the first two thirds of the poem, experience in the final third. And the parallels between the two parts make us wonder which is the greater innocence, Jane's as she remembers the way Philip used to flit in and out of her dress and press his bill between her lips, or the poet's as he longs to kiss her sugared mouth. In either case 'The matter were too nice:/And yet there was no vice,/Nor yet no villainy,/But only fantasy'. In its blurring of these extremes of the human state *Philip*

Sparrow looks forward to Andrew Marvell's *The Nymph Complaining for the Death of her Fawn* and William Blake's *Songs of Innocence and Experience.*

The other major Skeltonic in this selection is *The Tunning of Elinour Rumming*, and like most of Skelton's poems its fate has been to have had its complexities simplified out of existence. It is, as it has always been taken to be, a series of misogynist vignettes, showing Elinour's customers as variously stinking, half-naked, scurvy, deformed, impoverished, incoherent, and incontinent (most with a combination of these virtues), and the Skeltonic's exuberance gives the caricatures a grotesque force: 'Thither cometh Kate,/ Cicely and Sarah,/With their legs bare,/And also their feet/Hardly full unsweet;' 'With that her head shaked,/And her hands quaked—/ One's head would have ached/To see her naked;' 'There was a prick-me-dainty/ Sat like a sainty/ And began to painty/ As though she would fainty.' But there is more than merely affected distaste in Skelton's closing claim that he has 'written too much/Of this mad mumming/Of Elinour Rumming.' The clarion call to the drinking house—'Come whoso will'—is meant literally: the only bar to service is lack of the wherewithal to pay for Elinour's nappy ale, but the means of payment does not have to be money. Cicely and Sarah are the first of her customers prepared to pawn the ragged clothes they stand in for a drink; 'thus beginneth the game,' and the game is revealed throughout the poem as one of a society bent on pawning everything for drink. The list includes skillets, pots, a wedding ring, a husband's hood, spinning and weaving instruments, a good brass pan, gammon, bacon, cheese, a ladle, a cradle, and a side-saddle; and to those who have neither money nor goods to pay with Elinour ironically swears by the Lord who paid for her soul that they shall have nothing: 'Ye shall not bear away/ Mine ale for nought,/ By him that me bought!' (as in many of Skelton's poems there is a counterpoint of everyday oaths to offer a commentary on the action)—but by the poem's end even they have a prospect of liquid oblivion if they are prepared to chalk up their debt on Elinour's tally. (*Elinour Rumming* is not simply the transparent poem which C.S.Lewis held it to be: to read it is to experience the poet's alienation from a world of inebriates, and our alienation is most complete when we see the

14

word 'sport' (l.574) used as a jolly euphemism for spewing and excreting.

The dramatic presentation of alienation is an important element in two more of the longer poems in this selection, *The Bouge of Court* and *Speak, Parrot*. I stress 'dramatic' because it is worth remembering that Skelton's *Magnificence* has its prime place in the English morality play tradition as much for its dramatic power as for its moral vision. The most probable dating for *Magnificence* is 1515-18, in which case *The Bouge of Court* antedates it by almost twenty years, thereby demonstrating a continuing fascination felt by Skelton both for dramatic form and for the exposing of courtly hypocrisy. The poem begins as a dream vision, but as soon as the narrator is identified as Drede, in his dream state at least, and is taken on board the great courtly ship, its form shifts towards dramatic conflict and confrontation; and the great alienating factor so far as Drede is concerned is his inability to cope with the language of the men of court. Being a normal sane man Drede uses language to communicate; they use it for every other purpose but that, and one of the lessons Drede learns is that the most threatening words are a cover for inaction, while the most placatory promise imminent violence. Our share in the action is to perceive a poet finding, for the only time between Chaucer and the late Elizabethan dramatists, a way of absorbing contemporary idiom into verse: 'Spake he, a'faith, no word to you of me?' 'Sir, pardon me, I am an homely knave.' 'But no force, I shall once meet with thee.' 'Fie on these dice, they be not worth a turd!' 'I would each man were as plain as I./ It is a world, I say, to hear of some.'

Speak, Parrot has speaking parts too, but here the drama lies in the more concentrated form of a monologue. Parrot is the opposite of Drede, a character so cunning that he can find a multiplicity of bizarre ways to say a thing without appearing to say it, or not to say a thing while appearing to do so. Presumably his home now, since his exile from paradise, is a cage at court, in which case his ability to parrot nonsense is what keeps his head on his shoulders (parrots may not have shoulders but poets do). But a parrot in a cage is the original recording device, and Galathea, the one lady at court who realises this, sets herself to make Parrot speak out loud and clear.

Speak, Parrot is Skelton's most profound exploration of how a poet finds a language to suit the times, and the reader who holds on tight will find himself on one of the great switchback rides of English poetry. As well as Latin and Greek—one of the poem's major targets is the rise of humanist learning—languages as diverse as French, Spanish, Italian, German, Welsh, and Irish contribute to Parrot's prating, as well as snatches of popular song, the sophisticated terms of rhetoric and logic, the chatter of court ladies and politicians, and Biblical place and character names: all creating a poetry as allusive as T. S. Eliot thought only modern poetry could be to mirror the complexities of the twentieth century. But the early sixteenth century's complexities are Skelton's subject, and they consist of vast political, religious, and cultural shifts. On the eve of the Reformation and the Renaissance England is ruled by the son of an Ipswich butcher when it should be ruled by Skelton's former pupil—'Christ save King Henry the Eighth, our royal king'—its hold on the Catholic faith is weakening in the face of seductive Continental heresies, and its cultural system based on grammar and logic is giving way to a new learning. For an old poet (Skelton is now in his sixties) the result is an anarchy and chaos which only a parrot's lunacy can convey. Through the caged bird, with his silver pin and pretty mirror, England becomes the Israel of the unheard prophets: Jeremiah weeps in Heshbon as Jephthah lies dead, and Og the king of Bashan triumphs—and Heshbon is set alongside Marylebone and Whetstone next Barnet in Skelton's Blakean topography.

Galathea's method of getting Parrot to speak out plainly is to make him see the implications of Wolsey's inflationary policies. In the poem's first stanza Parrot's reward for his prattling is to have 'an almond or a date'. Many stanzas later Galathea forces him to acknowledge that 'dates now are dainty, and wax very scant', and in a series of magnificent food-centred puns Parrot sees the scantness of raisins and dates as the last symptom in the body politic's decay:

> Now, Galathea, let Parrot, I pray you have his date—
> Yet dates now are dainty, and wax very scant,
> For grocers were grudged at and groaned at but late;
> Great raisins with reasons be now reprobitant,

For raisins are no reasons, but reasons currant.
Run God, run Devil! Yet the date of our Lord
And the date of the Devil doth surely accord.

A poem which had opened with cloaked allusion and catching the sense at two removes now closes with the most transparently clear descriptions imaginable. In Parrot's plain speaking every line makes its point, whether it be to show the divide between rich and poor—'So gorgeous garments, and so much wretchedness'—or to sum up the one man responsible for the country's situation—'So much of "my Lord's grace", and in him no grace is'—or to describe what it is like to live in a police state—'So much privy watching in cold winters' nights'.

Quod scripsi, scripsi—'What I have written I have written'—wrote Skelton in *The Garland of Laurel*, and it was a summary of defeat and victory. In the short term Wolsey won: he silenced Skelton's satire, and even exacted an obsequious compliment from him; and in the long term the Renaissance and the Reformation won too—both defeats for Skelton. But *The Garland of Laurel* is a claim to poetic immortality, the literal crowning of the poet laureate with the laurel wreath, and it represents victory on many levels. Wolsey is reminded that what poets write lasts, while corrupt statesmen and churchmen are soon remembered only as rabid dogs; and in the longer term there is a more subtle and more moving victory, for Skelton throws down a challenge to the whole English Renaissance. Whether, as has been argued, the *Garland* was actually begun in the fifteenth century, and taken up again by the ageing poet twenty years later, it still stands as the last great English medieval poem. Here the dream vision, the Queen of Fame, Dame Pallas, Gower, Chaucer, and Lydgate reach into the sixteenth century with a fullness of creative assurance not to be found again by English poets for sixty years. In this poem, as in the others in this selection, Skelton shows what English poetry might have been had it not succumbed to Italy and the new learning. The rhyme royal stanzas sustain both an artificial richness of description and the natural vigour of human expression, and set into the poem is a series of lyrics to the ladies who weave his garland which rivals anything the Elizabethan lyricists were to achieve.

17

The battle to win Skelton's long term reputation continues. Despite the loud praise of twentieth century poets like Graves and Auden, there is not, as I write this, any edition of his poems in print in England. Something similar happened in the sixteenth century. Skelton's popular reputation diminished until he had become, by the end of the century, the merry, mad 'hero' of Elizabethan jest books; but the poets, like Spenser and Jonson, knew his value, and when Michael Drayton wanted to write a poem on the subject of poetic immortality he chose, fittingly, to call it a Skeltoniad and to write it in the Skeltonic form. Towards its close it has lines which make a fitting epitaph to Skelton's life and work:

> Parnassus is not clome,
> By every such mome;
> Up whose steep side who swerves
> It behoves to have strong nerves.

Skelton's satirical verse bears witness to his 'strong nerves', but I should like to close this introduction by emphasising one other way in which the phrase is relevant, and that is to the verbal sinews of his poetry. Reading Skelton is a constant challenge to one's linguistic perceptions: in nearly every line, certainly in every stanza or paragraph, he stretches the language. You can test that on the levels of syntax, rhythm, and rhyme, by opening this book at any page of the text. For instance, a short poem like *The Ancient Acquaintance* (p. 24) begins with the detached elegance of courtly compliment addressed to a lady, with rhythm and syntax to match; then it shifts in the middle stanzas into a vision of the lady's uncontrollable sexual frenzy and her cuckolded husband's rage, again matched in the poem's expression; and it closes with the cool voice of the poet warning that unless she changes her behaviour he will spill the beans. What the modern reader may miss, though, is the word-play by means of which Skelton identifies the lady's lust with that of a mare in heat: through the third and fourth stanzas her actions and the mare's are given in a series of punning parallels, just as the poem's rhythm in this part conveys the wanton excitability of such a creature.

An editor who tried to explain all such word games in Skelton's poetry would end up with a monster set of notes and glossary, and that would have quite the wrong effect, for so fresh a poet should

18

not be swamped in scholarship. In other words, the reader of this selection should keep his wits about him for a poet whose verbal ambushes are everywhere. Most, fortunately, have not withered with age. To take one example, when Parrot wants to convey the style of Wolsey's political machinations he does so by casting him as a card sharper: first in a visual pun of Wolsey with 'a king in his sleeve', and then in the pure language pun of 'chief cardinal' and 'chief card in all'. And the reader ought also to be aware that his perplexities are not necessarily very far removed from the responses of Skelton's contemporaries. Shakespeare apart, and that is a dubious exception, there is no English poet who coined so many words and meanings. The *New English Dictionary* credits him with first using, either completely or in special senses, 640 words, and the editors of his prose translation of *The Bibliotheca Historica of Diodorus Siculus* have been able to add over 800 to that list. Perhaps some of these are explainable as first recorded uses of words long existing but never till then written down in anything which has survived; but the impression is still of a constant innovating force—*blommer, bullifant, emportured, pendugum, versing-box*, any or all might well have struck Skelton's contemporary reader as an expansion of his language. All the modern dictionary and glossary maker can do is to render their meanings as 'obscure' and their first, and often only, user as Skelton. But they are only dead specimens for lexicographers; for readers they have all the sinewy life which a poem can give them. To return to our beginning, the laureate garment which Skelton wore was probably coloured green, and green is the triumphant colour of *The Garland of Laurel* and *Calliope*. Even though the poet's words may, like his body, 'wax old/ And somedele sere,' wrap them in their proper covering and they stay young.

WOEFULLY ARRAYED

Woefully arrayed,
   My blood, man,
   For thee ran,
It may not be nayed:
   My body blo and wan,
Woefully arrayed.

Behold me, I pray thee, with all thy whole reason,
And be not so hard-hearted, and for this encheason,
Sith I for thy soul sake was slain in good season,
Beguiled and betrayed by Judas' false treason;
   Unkindly entreated,
   With sharp cord sore freted,
   The Jews me threted:
They mowed, they grinned, they scorned me,
Condemned to death, as thou mayest see,
   Woefully arrayed.

Thus naked am I nailed, O man, for thy sake:
I love thee, then love me; why sleepest thou? awake!
Remember my tender heart-root for thee brake,
With pains my veins constrained to crake:
   Thus tugged to and fro,
   Thus wrapped all in woe,
   Whereas never man was so
Entreated thus in most cruel wise,
Was like a lamb offered in sacrifice,
   Woefully arrayed.

Of sharp thorn I have worn a crown on my head,
So pained, so strained, so rueful, so red,
Thus bobbed, thus robbed, thus for thy love dead,
Unfeigned not deigned my blood for to shed:
   My feet and hands sore
   The sturdy nails bore:

What might I suffer more
Than I have done, O man, for thee?
Come when thou list, welcome to me,
    Woefully arrayed.

Of record thy good Lord I have been and shall be;
I am thine, thou art mine, my brother I call thee;
Thee love I entirely—see what is befall me:
40   Sore beating, sore threating, to make thee, man, all free.
    Why art thou unkind?
    Why hast not me in mind?
    Come yet and thou shalt find
  Mine endless mercy and grace.
  See how a spear my heart did race,
    Woefully arrayed.

Dear brother, no other thing I of thee desire
But give me thine heart free to reward mine hire:
I wrought thee, I bought thee from eternal fire:
50   I pray thee array thee toward my high empire
    Above the orient,
    Whereof I am regent,
    Lord God omnipotent,
  With me to reign in endless wealth:
  Remember, man, thy soul's health.

    Woefully arrayed,
      My blood, man,
      For thee ran,
    It may not be nayed:
60   My blood blo and wan,
    Woefully arrayed.

MY DARLING DEAR, MY DAISY FLOWER

With lullay, lullay, like a child,
Thou sleepest too long, thou art beguiled.

'My darling dear, my daisy flower,
Let me', quoth he, 'lie in your lap'.
'Lie still', quoth she, 'my paramour,
Lie still hardely, and take a nap'.
His head was heavy, such was his hap,
All drowsy, dreaming, drowned in sleep,
That of his love he took no keep.
 With hey lullay, lullay, like a child,
  Thou sleepest too long, thou art beguiled.

With 'ba, ba, ba', and 'bas, bas, bas',
She cherished him both cheek and chin,
That he wist never where he was;
He had forgotten all deadly sin.
He wanted wit her love to win:
He trusted her payment and lost all his prey;
She left him sleeping and stole away.
 With hey lullay, lullay, like a child,
  Thou sleepest too long, thou art beguiled.

The rivers rowth, the waters wan,
She spared not to wet her feet.
She waded over, she found a man
That halsed her heartily and kissed her sweet;
Thus after her cold she caught a heat.
'My lefe', she said, 'routeth in his bed;
Ywis he hath an heavy head'.
 With hey lullay, lullay, like a child,
  Thou sleepest too long, thou art beguiled.

What dreamest thou, drunkard, drowsy pate?
Thy lust and liking is from thee gone;

Thou blinkard blowboll, thou wakest too late:
Behold thou liest, luggard, alone.
Well may thou sigh, well may thou groan,
To deal with her so cowardly:
Ywis, pole hatchet, she bleared thine eye!

THE ANCIENT ACQUAINTANCE, MADAM,
BETWEEN US TWAIN

The ancient acquaintance, madam, between us twain,
The familiarity, the former dalliance,
Causeth me that I cannot myself refrain
But that I must write for my pleasant pastance:
Remembering your passing goodly countenance,
Your goodly port, your beauteous visage,
Ye may be counted comfort of all courage.

Of all your features favourable to make true description,
I am insufficient to make such enterprise
10   For this dare I say, without tradition,
That Dame Menolope was never half so wise.
Yet so it is that a rumour beginneth so to rise,
How in good horsemen ye set your whole delight,
And have forgotten your old true loving knight.

With bound and rebound, bouncingly take up
His gentle curtal, and set nought by small nags.
Spur up at the hinder girth, with 'gup, morell, gup!'
With 'jayst ye, jennet of Spain, for your tail wags!'
Ye cast all your courage upon such courtly hags.
20   'Have in sergeant farrier, mine horse behind is bare';
He rideth well the horse, but he rideth better the mare.

Ware, ware the mare winceth with her wanton heel!
She kicketh with her calkins and keyleth with a clench;
She goeth wide behind, and hueth never a deal:

24

Ware galling in the withers, ware of that wrench!
It is perilous for a horseman to dig in the trench.
This grieveth your husband, that right gentle knight,
And so with your servants he fiercely doth fight.

So fiercely he fighteth, his mind is so fell,
30   That he driveth them down with dints on their day-watch.
He bruiseth their brainpans and maketh them to swell.
Their brows all to-broken, such claps they catch;
Whose jealousy malicious maketh them to leap the hatch,
By their cognizance knowing how they serve a wily pie:
Ask all your neighbours whether that I lie.

It can be no counsel that is cried at the cross;
For your gentle husband sorrowful am I.
Howbeit, he is not first hath had a loss.
Advertising you, madam, to work more secretly.
40   Let not all the world make an outcry:
Play fair play, madam, and look ye play clean,
Or else with great shame your game will be seen.

MANNERLY MARGERY MILK AND ALE

Ay, beshrew you, by my fay,
These wanton clerks be nice alway;
Avaunt, avaunt, my popagay!
What, will ye do nothing but play?
Tilly vally, straw, let be I say.
Gup, Christian Clout, gup, Jack of the Vale!
With Mannerly Margery Milk and Ale.

By God, ye be a pretty pode,
And I love you an whole cart load.
10   Straw, James Fodder, ye play the fode,
I am no hackney for your rod:
Go watch a bull, your back is broad.

Gup, Christian Clout, gup, Jack of the Vale!
With Mannerly Margery Milk and Ale.

Ywis ye deal uncourteously;
What, would ye frumple me? now fie!
What, and ye shall be my pig's eye?
By Christ, ye shall not, no hardely:
I will not be japed bodily.
20   Gup, Christian Clout, gup, Jack of the Vale!
With Mannerly Margery Milk and Ale.

Walk forth your way, ye cost me nought;
Now have I found that I have sought,
The best cheap flesh that ever I bought.
Yet, for His love that all hath wrought,
Wed me, or else I die for thought.
Gup, Christian Clout, your breath is stale!
Go, Mannerly Margery Milk and Ale!
Gup, Christian Clout, gup, Jack of the Vale!
30   With Mannerly Margery Milk and Ale.

WOMANHOOD, WANTON, YE WANT

Womanhood, wanton, ye want:
Your meddling, mistress, is mannerless;
Plenty of ill, of goodness scant,
Ye rail at riot, reckless.
To praise your port it is needless;
For all your 'draff' yet and your 'dregs,'
As well borne as ye full oft times begs.

Why so coy and full of scorn?
'Mine horse is sold, I ween,' you say;
10   'My new furred gown, when it is worn—
Put up your purse, ye shall none pay!'
By creed, I trust to see the day,

As proud a pea-hen as ye spread:
Of me and other ye may have need!

Though angelic be your smiling,
Yet is your tongue an adder's tail,
Full like a scorpion stinging
All those by whom ye have avail.
Good mistress Anne, there ye do shail:
20   What prate ye, pretty pig's eye?
I trust to quit you or I die!

Your key is meet for every lock,
Your key is common and hangeth out;
Your key is ready, we need not knock,
Nor stand long wresting thereabout;
Of your door-gate ye have no doubt.
But one thing is, that ye be lewd:
Hold your tongue now, all beshrewed.

To Mistress Anne, that farly sweet,
30   That wones at The Key in Thames Street.

from THE BOUGE OF COURT

1-182: The poet contemplates his own inadequacy 'to touch a truth
and cloak it subtly' when compared with the achievements of 'poets
old'. Depressed at this he falls asleep in a Harwich inn. He dreams of
a great ship whose name is 'The Bouge of Court'; its owner is Dame
Sanspeer. When challenged the poet identifies himself as 'Drede'
(i.e. Dread). Drede meets the first of his fellow travellers Favell
(flattery), who assures him that he is sufficiently in Fortune's favour
to overcome the enemies who surround him. As Favell leaves he has
words with another passenger, Suspect.

'In faith,' quoth Suspect, 'spake Drede no word of me?'
'Why? what then? wilt thou let men to speak?
He saith he cannot well accord with thee.'

'Twist,' quoth Suspect, 'go play, him I ne reke.'
'By Christ,' quoth Favell, 'Drede is sullen freke.
What, let us hold him up, man, for a while.'
'Yes so,' quoth Suspect, 'he may us both beguile.'

190   And when he came walking soberly,
With 'hum' and 'ha' and with a crooked look,
Methought his head was full of jealousy,
His eyen rolling, his hands fast they quoke;
And to meward the straight way he took.
'God speed, brother,' to me quoth he then,
And thus to talk with me he began.

Suspicion
'Ye remember the gentleman right now
That communed with you, methought a pretty space?
Beware of him, for, I make God avow,
200   He will beguile you and speak fair to your face.
Ye never dwelt in such another place,
For here is none that dare well other trust—
But I would tell you a thing, and I durst.

'Spake he, a'faith, no word to you of me?
I wot, and he did, ye would me tell.
I have a favour to you, whereof it be
That I must show you much of my counsel—
But I wonder what the devil of hell
He said of me, when he with you did talk—
210   By mine advice use not with him to walk.

'The sovereignest thing that any man may have
Is little to say, and much to hear and see;
For, but I trusted you, so God me save,
I would nothing so plain be:
To you only, methink, I durst shrive me,
For now am I plenarly disposed
To show you things that may not be disclosed.'

Drede
Then I assured him my fidelity
His counsel secret never to discure,
220 If he could find in heart to trust me;
Else I prayed him, with all my busy cure,
To keep it himself, for then he might be sure
That no man earthly could him bewray,
Whiles of his mind it were locked with the key.

'By God,' quoth he, 'this and thus it is;'
And of his mind he showed me all and some.
'Farewell,' quoth he, 'we will talk more of this.'
So he departed; there he would come
I dare not speak—I promised to be dumb.
230 But, as I stood musing in my mind,
Harvy Hafter came leaping, light as lynde.

Upon his breast he bare a versing-box,
His throat was clear, and lustily could fain.
Methought his gown was all furred with fox,
And ever he sang, 'Sith I am nothing plain . . .'
To keep him from picking it was a great pain;
He gazed on me with his goatish beard,
When I looked on him my purse was half afeared.

Harvy Hafter
'Sir, God you save, why look ye so sad?
240 What thing is that I may do for you?
A wonder thing that ye wax not mad!
For, and I study should as ye do now,
My wit would waste, I make God avow.
Tell me your mind: methink ye make a verse;
I could it scan, and ye would it rehearse.

'But to the point shortly to proceed,
Where hath your dwelling been ere ye came here?
For, as I trow, I have seen you indeed

Ere this, when that ye made me royal cheer.
250 Hold up the helm, look up, and let God steer:
I would be merry that wind that ever blow!
Heave and ho, rumbelow, row the boat, Norman, row!

'*Princes of Youth* can ye sing by rote?
Or *Shall I sail with you* a fellowship assay?
For on the book I cannot sing a note.
Would to God, it would please you some day
A ballad book before me for to lay,
And learn me to sing *re mi fa sol*,
And, when I fail, bob me on the noll.

260 'Lo, what is to you a pleasure great
To have that cunning and ways that ye have!
By God's soul, I wonder how ye gat
So great pleasure, or who to you it gave.
Sir, pardon me, I am an homely knave,
To be with you thus pert and thus bold;
But ye be welcome to our household.

'And, I dare say, there is no man herein
But would be glad of your company.
I wist never man that so soon could win
270 The favour that ye have with my lady.
I pray to God that it may never die.
It is your fortune for to have that grace—
As I be saved, it is a wonder case!

'For, as for me, I served here many a day,
And yet unneth I can have my living:
But, I require you, no word that I say!
For, and I know any earthly thing
That is again you, ye shall have weeting.
And ye be welcome, sir, so God me save,
280 I hope hereafter a friend of you to have.'

30

Drede
With that, as he departed so from me,
Anon there met with him, as methought,
A man, but wonderly beseen was he.
He looked haughty; he set each man at nought;
His gaudy garment with scorns was all wrought;
With indignation lined was his hood;
He frowned as he would swear by Cock's blood.

He bit the lip, he looked passing coy;
His face was belimmed, as bees had him stung:
290   It was no time with him to jape nor toy.
Envy hath wasted his liver and his lung,
Hatred by the heart so had him wrung
That he looked pale as ashes to my sight.
Disdain, I ween, this cumbrous carcass hight.

To Harvy Hafter then he spake of me,
And I drew near to hark what they two said.
'Now,' quoth Disdain, 'as I shall saved be,
I have great scorn, and am right evil apayed.'
'Then,' quoth Harvy, 'why art thou so dismayed?'
300   'By Christ,' quoth he, 'for it is shame to say,
To see Johan Dawes, that came but yesterday,

'How he is now taken in conceit,
This Doctor Dawcock, Drede, I ween he hight.
By God's bones, but if we have some slight,
It is like he will stand in our light.'
'By God,' quoth Harvy, 'and it so happen might.
Let us therefore shortly at a word
Find some mean to cast him over the board.'

'By Him that me bought,' then quoth Disdain,
310   'I wonder sore he is in such conceit.'
'Turd!' quoth Hafter, 'I will thee nothing layne,
There must for him be laid some pretty bait.
We twain, I trow, be not without deceit:

First pick a quarrel, and fall out with him then,
And so outface him with a card of ten.'

Forthwith he made on me a proud assault,
With scornful look moved all in mood.
He went about to take me in a fault:
He frowned, he stared, he stamped where he stood:
320 I looked on him, I weened he had been wood.
He set the arm proudly under the side,
And in this wise he 'gan with me to chide.

Disdain
'Rememberest thou what thou said yesternight?
Wilt thou abide by thy words again?
By God, I have of thee now great despite;
I shall thee anger once in every vein!
It is great scorn to see such an hayne
As thou art, one that came but yesterday,
With us old servants such masters to play.

330 'I tell thee, I am of countenance;
What weenest I were? I trow thou know not me!
By God's wounds, but for displeasance,
Of my quarrel soon would I venged be.
But, no force, I shall once meet with thee:
Come when it will, oppose thee I shall,
Whatsomever adventure thereof fall.

'Trowest thou, drevill, I say, thou gaudy knave,
That I have deinte to see thee cherished thus?
By God's side, my sword thy beard shall shave!
340 Well, once thou shalt be charmed, ywis—
Nay, straw for tales, thou shalt not rule us:
We be thy betters, and so thou shalt us take,
Or we shall thee out of thy clothes shake!'

Drede

With that came Riot, rushing all at once,
A rusty gallant, to-ragged and to-rent;
And on the board he whirled a pair of bones,
Quater trey deuce he clattered as he went.
'Now have at all, by Saint Thomas of Kent!'
And ever he threw and cast I wote ne'er what:
350   His hair was grown through out his hat.

Then I beheld how he disguised was:
His head was heavy for watching overnight,
His eyen bleared, his face shone like a glass;
His gown so short that it ne cover might
His rump, he went so all for summer light.
His hose was garded with a list of green,
Yet at the knee they were broken, I ween.

His coat was checked with patches red and blue;
Of Kirby Kendal was his short demi;
360   And aye he sang, 'In faith, deacon, thou crew.'
His elbow bare, he wore his gear so nigh,
His nose a-dropping, his lips were full dry;
And by his side his whinard and his pouch,
The devil might dance therein for any crowch.

Counter he could *O lux* upon a pot,
An ostrich feather of a capon's tail
He set up freshly upon his hat aloft.
'What revel rout!' quoth he, and 'gan to rail
How oft he had hit Jennet on the tail
370   Of Phyllis feateous, and little pretty Kate,
How oft he knocked at her clicket-gate.

What should I tell more of his ribaldry?
I was ashamed so to hear him prate;
He had no pleasure but in harlotry.
'Ay,' quoth he, 'in the devil's date

What art thou? I saw thee now but late.'
'Forsooth,' quoth I, 'in this court I dwell now.'
'Welcome,' quoth Riot, 'I make God avow.

Riot
'And, sir, in faith why com'st not us among
380 To make thee merry, as other fellows done?
Thou must swear and stare, man, all day long,
And wake all night, and sleep till it be noon;
Thou mayest not study, or muse on the moon;
This world is nothing but eat, drink, and sleep,
And thus with us good company to keep.

'Pluck up thine heart upon a merry pin,
And let us laugh a plack or twain at nale:
What the devil, man, mirth is here within!
What, lo man, see here of dice a bale;
390 A bridling-cast for that is in thy male!
Now have at all that lieth upon the board—
Fie on these dice, they be not worth a turd!

'Have at the hazard, or at the dozen brown,
Or else I pass a penny to a pound!
Now would to God thou would lay money down:
Lord, how that I would cast it full round!
Ay, in my pouch a buckle I have found—
The arms of Calais, I have no coin nor cross:
I am not happy, I run aye on the loss.

400 'Now run must I to the stew's side
To weet if Malkin, my lemman, have got ought:
I let her to hire, that men may on her ride,
Her arms easy far and near is sought:
By God's side, since I her thither brought
She hath got me more money with her tail
Than hath some ship that into Bordeaux sail.

34

'Had I as good an horse as she is a mare,
I durst adventure to journey through France;
Who rideth on her, he needeth not to care,
410 For she is trussed for to break a lance:
It is a curtal that well can winch and prance.
To her will I now all my poverty ledge,
And, till I come, have here mine hat to pledge.'

Drede
Gone is this knave, this ribald foul and lewd.
He ran as fast as ever that he might.
Unthriftiness in him may well be showed,
For whom Tyburn groaneth both day and night.
And, as I stood and cast aside my sight,
Disdain I saw with Dissimulation
420 Standing in sad communication.

But there was pointing and nodding with the head,
And many words said in secret wise;
They wandered aye, and stood still in no stead:
Methought alway Dissimuler did devise.
Me passing sore mine heart then 'gan arise;
I deemed and dread their talking was not good.
Anon Dissimuler came where I stood.

Then in his hood I saw there faces twain:
That one was lean and like a pined ghost,
430 That other looked as he would me have slain;
And to meward as he 'gan for to coast,
When that he was even at me almost,
I saw a knife hid in his one sleeve,
Whereon was written this word, *Mischief*.

And in his other sleeve methought I saw
A spoon of gold, full of honey sweet,
To feed a fool, and for to prey a daw;
And on that sleeve these words were writ,

A false abstract cometh from a false concrete.
400 His hood was side, his cope was russet grey:
These were the words that he to me did say.

Dissimulation
'How do ye, master? ye look so soberly.
As I be saved at the dreadful day,
It is a perilous vice, this envy.
Alas, a cunning man ne dwell may
In no place well, but fools with him fray.
But as for that, cunning hath no foe
Save him that nought can: Scripture saith so.

'I know your virtue and your literature
450 By that little cunning that I have:
Ye be maligned sore, I you ensure;
But ye have craft yourself alway to save.
It is great scorn to see a misproud knave
With a clerk that cunning is to prate:
Let them go louse them, in the devil's date!

'For albeit that this long not to me,
Yet on my back I bear such lewd dealing:
Right now I spake with one, I trow, I see—
But, what, a straw! I may not tell all thing.
460 By God, I say there is great heart-burning
Between the person ye wot of, you—
Alas, I could not deal so with a Jew!

'I would each man were as plain as I.
It is a world, I say, to hear of some:
I hate this feigning, fie upon it, fie!
A man cannot wot where to be come.
Ywis I could tell—but humlery, hum!
I dare not speak, we be so laid await,
For all our court is full of deceit.

470 'Now by Saint Francis, that holy man and friar,
I hate these ways again you that they take!
Were I as you, I would ride them full near,
And, by my troth, but if an end they make,
Yet will I say some words for your sake
That shall them anger, I hold thereon a groat:
For some shall ween be hanged by the throat!

'I have a stopping oyster in my poke,
Trust me, and if it come to a need;
But I am loath for to raise a smoke,
480 If ye could be otherwise agreed.
And so I would it were, so God me speed,
For this may breed to a confusion
Without God make a good conclusion.

'Nay, see where yonder standeth the tother man:
A flattering knave and false he is, God wot;
The drevil standeth to hearken, and he can
It were more thrift he bought him a new coat;
It will not be, his purse is not on float:
All that he weareth, it is borrowed ware,
490 His wit is thin, his hood is threadbare.

'More could I say, but what this is enow;
Adieu till soon, we shall speak more of this.
Ye must be ruled as I shall tell you how;
Amends may be of that is now amiss.
And I am your, sir, so have I bliss,
In every point that I can do or say.
Give me your hand, farewell, and have good day.'

Drede
Suddenly, as he departed me fro,
Came pressing in one in a wonder array.
500 Ere I was aware, behind me he said 'Boo!'
Then I, astonied of that sudden fray,

Start all at once. I liked nothing his play:
For, if I had not quickly fled the touch,
He had plucked out the nobles of my pouch.

He was trussed in a garment straight;
I had not seen such another's page,
For he could well upon a casket wait;
His hood all pounsed and garded like a cage;
Light lime-finger, he took none other wage.
510 'Hearken,' quoth he, 'lo, here mine hand in thine:
To us welcome thou art, by Saint Quintin.'

Deceit
'But, by that Lord that is one, two, and three,
I have an errand to round in your ear.
He told me so, by God, ye may trust me:
Parde, remember when ye were there,
There I winked on you—wot ye not where?
In A loco, I mean *juxta B:*
Woe is him that is blind and may not see!

'But to hear the subtlety and the craft,
520 As I shall tell you, if ye will hear again:
And, when I saw the whoresons would you haft,
To hold mine hand, by God, I had great pain;
For forthwith there I had him slain,
But that I dread murder would come out;
Who dealeth with shrews hath need to look about!

Drede
And as he rounded thus in mine ear
Of false collusion confettered by assent,
Methought I see lewd fellows here and there
Come for to slay me of mortal intent.
530 And, as they came, the shipboard fast I hent,
And thought to leap, and even with that woke,
Caught pen and ink, and wrote this little book.

I would therewith no man were miscontent,
Beseeching you that shall it see or read
In every point to be indifferent,
Sith all in substance of slumbering doth proceed.
I will not say it is matter indeed,
But yet oft-time such dreams be found true.
Now construe ye what is the residue.

PHILIP SPARROW

Pla ce bo,
    Who is there, who?
Di le xi,
    Dame Margery,
Fa, re, my, my,
    Wherefore and why, why?
    For the soul of Philip Sparrow
That was late slain at Carrow,
Among the Nuns Black.
For that sweet soul's sake,
And for all sparrows' souls
Set in our bead-rolls,
Pater noster qui,
With an *Ave Mari*,
And with the corner of a Creed,
The more shall be your meed.

    When I remember again
How my Philip was slain,
Never half the pain
Was between you twain,
Pyramus and Thisbe,
As then befell to me.
I wept and I wailed,
The tears down hailed,
But nothing it availed

39

To call Philip again,
Whom Gib our cat hath slain.
   Gib, I say, our cat
Worrowed her on that
Which I loved best.
It cannot be expressed
My sorrowful heaviness,
But all without redress;
For within that stound,
Half slumbering, in a sound
I fell down to the ground.

   Unneth I cast mine eyes
Toward the cloudy skies;
But when I did behold
My sparrow dead and cold,
No creature but that would
Have rued upon me
To behold and see
What heaviness did me pang:
Wherewith my hands I wrang,
That my sinews cracked
As though I had been racked,
So pained and so strained
That no life well nigh remained.

   I sighed and I sobbed,
For that I was robbed
Of my sparrow's life.
O maiden, widow, and wife,
Of what estate ye be,
Of high or low degree,
Great sorrow then ye might see,
And learn to weep at me!
Such pains did me frete
That mine heart did beat,
My visage pale and dead,
Wan, and blue as lead:

The pangs of hateful death
Well nigh had stopped my breath.

    Heu, heu, me,
That I am woe for thee!
Ad Dominum, cum tribularer, clamavi.
Of God nothing else crave I
But Philip's soul to keep
From the marees deep
70   Of Acherontes' well,
That is a flood of hell;
And from the great Pluto,
The prince of endless woe;
And from foul Alecto,
With visage black and blue;
And from Medusa that mare,
That like a fiend doth stare;
And from Megaera's adders
For ruffling of Philip's feathers,
80   And from her fiery sparklings
For burning of his wings;
And from the smokes sour
Of Proserpina's bower;
And from the dens dark
Where Cerberus doth bark,
Whom Theseus did affray,
Whom Hercules did outray,
As famous poets say;
From that hell hound
90   That lieth in chains bound,
With ghastly heads three;
To Jupiter pray we
That Philip preserved may be.
Amen, say ye with me!
    Do mi nus,
       Help now sweet Jesus!
    Levavi oculos meos in montes.

Would God I had Xenophontes,
Or Socrates the wise,
100 To show me their device
Moderately to take
This sorrow that I make
For Philip Sparrow's sake.
So fervently I shake,
I feel my body quake;
So urgently I am brought
Into careful thought.
Like Andromache, Hector's wife,
Was weary of her life,
110 When she had lost her joy,
Noble Hector of Troy;
In like manner also
Increaseth my deadly woe,
For my sparrow is go.
 It was so pretty a fool,
It would sit on a stool,
And learned after my school
For to keep his cut,
With 'Philip, keep your cut.'
120 It had a velvet cap,
And would sit upon my lap,
And seek after small worms,
And sometime white bread-crumbs;
And many times and oft
Between my breasts soft
It would lie and rest;
It was proper and prest.
 Sometime he would gasp
When he saw a wasp;
130 A fly or a gnat,
He would fly at that,
And prettily he would pant
When he saw an ant.
Lord, how he would pry

42

After the butterfly!
Lord, how he would hop
After the gressop!
And when I said, 'Phip, Phip,'
Then he would leap and skip,
And take me by the lip.
Alas, it will me slo
That Philip is gone me fro
    Si in i qui ta tes
      Alas, I was evil at ease.
    De pro fun dis cla ma vi,
      When I saw my sparrow die.

    Now, after my doom,
Dame Sulpicia at Rome,
Whose name registered was
For ever in tables of brass,
Because that she did pass
In poesy to indite
And eloquently to write,
Though she would pretend
My sparrow to commend,
I trow she could not amend
Reporting the virtues all
Of my sparrow royal.
    For it would come and go,
And fly so to and fro;
And on me it would leap
When I was asleep,
And his feathers shake,
Wherewith he would make
Me often for to wake,
And for to take him in
Upon my naked skin.
God wot, we thought no sin:
What though he crept so low?
It was no hurt, I trow;

140
150
160
170

43

He did nothing, perdee,
But sit upon my knee.
Philip, though he were nice,
In him it was no vice.
Philip had leave to go
To pick my little toe:
Philip might be bold
And do what he would;
Philip would seek and take
180   All the fleas black
That he could there espy
With his wanton eye.

     O pe ra,
        La, sol, fa, fa,
       Confitebor tibi, Domine, in toto corde meo.
        Alas, I would ride and go
       A thousand mile of ground;
If any such might be found
It were worth an hundred pound
190   Of King Croesus' gold,
Or of Attalus the old,
The rich prince of Pergame,
Whoso list the story to see.
Cadmus, that his sister sought,
And he should be bought
For gold and fee,
He should over the sea
To weet if he could bring
Any of the offspring,
200   Or any of the blood.
But whoso understood
Of Medea's art,
I would I had a part
Of her crafty magic.
My sparrow then should be quick
With a charm or twain,
And play with me again.

But all this is in vain
Thus for to complain.
210   I took my sampler once
Of purpose, for the nonce,
To sew with stitches of silk
My sparrow white as milk,
That by representation
Of his image and fashion
To me it might import
Some pleasure and comfort,
For my solace and sport.
But when I was sewing his beak,
220 Methought my sparrow did speak,
And opened his pretty bill,
Saying, 'Maid, ye are in will
Again me for to kill,
Ye prick me in the head!'
With that my needle waxed red,
Methought, of Philip's blood;
Mine hair right upstood,
And was in such a fray
My speech was taken away.
230 I cast down that there was,
And said, 'Alas, alas,
How cometh this to pass?'
My fingers dead and cold
Could not my sampler hold;
My needle and thread
I threw away for dread.
The best now that I may
Is for his soul to pray:
     A porta inferi,
240   Good Lord, have mercy
Upon my sparrow's soul,
     Written in my bead-roll.
     Au di vi vo cem,
       Japhet, Ham, and Shem,

Ma gni fi cat,
> Show me the right path
> To the hills of Armony,
> Wherefore the boards yet cry
> Of your father's boat,

250 That was sometime afloat,
And now they lie and rot:
Let some poets write
Deucalion's flood it hight.
> But as verily as ye be
The natural sons three
Of Noah the patriarch,
That made that great ark,
Wherein he had apes and owls,
Beasts, birds, and fowls,

260 That if ye can find
Any of my sparrow's kind—
God send the soul good rest!
I would have yet a nest
As pretty and as prest
As my sparrow was.
But my sparrow did pass
All sparrows of the wood
That were since Noah's flood,
Was never none so good.

270 King Philip of Macedony
Had no such Philip as I,
No, no, sir, hardely!
> That vengeance I ask and cry,
By way of exclamation,
On all the whole nation
Of cats wild and tame:
God send them sorrow and shame!
That cat specially
That slew so cruelly

280 My little pretty sparrow
That I brought up at Carrow.

O cat of curlish kind,
The fiend was in thy mind
When thou my bird untwined:
I would thou hadst been blind!
The leopards savage,
The lions in their rage,
Might catch thee in their paws,
And gnaw thee in their jaws!
The serpents of Libany
Might sting thee venomously!
The dragons with their tongues
Might poison thy liver and lungs!
The manticors of the mountains
Might feed them on thy brains!
Melanchaetes, that hound
That plucked Actaeon to the ground,
Gave him his mortal wound,
Changed to a deer,
The story doth appear,
Was changed to an hart:
So thou, foul cat that thou art,
The selfsame hound
Might thee confound,
That his own lord bote,
Might bite asunder thy throat!
Of Ind the greedy grypes
Might tear out all thy tripes!
Of Arcady the bears
Might pluck away thine ears!
The wild wolf Lycaon
Bite asunder thy backbone!
Of Etna the burning hill,
That day and night burneth still,
Set in thy tail a blaze,
That all the world may gaze
And wonder upon thee,
From Ocean, the great sea,

Unto the Isles of Orcady,
From Tilbury Ferry
To the plain of Salisbury!
So traitorously my bird to kill
That never ought thee evil will!
　　Was never bird in cage
More gentle of courage
In doing his homage
Unto his sovereign.
Alas, I say again,
Death hath departed us twain:
The false cat hath thee slain!
Farewell, Philip, adieu;
Our Lord, thy soul rescue.
Farewell, without restore;
Farewell, for evermore.
　　And it were a jew,
It would make one rue,
To see my sorrow new.
These villainous false cats
Were made for mice and rats,
And not for birds small.
Alas, my face waxeth pale,
Telling this piteous tale,
How my bird so fair,
That was wont to repair,
And go in at my spair,
And creep in at my gore
Of my gown before,
Flickering with his wings—
Alas, my heart it stings,
Remembering pretty things!
Alas, mine heart it slaith,
My Philip's doleful death!
When I remember it,
How prettily it would sit,
Many times and oft

320

330

340

350

Upon my finger aloft.
I played with him tittle-tattle,
And fed him with my spittle,
With his bill between my lips,
360   It was my pretty Phips!
Many a pretty kiss
Had I of his sweet muss!
And now the cause is thus,
That he is slain me fro,
To my great pain and woe.
        Of Fortune this the chance
Standeth on variance:
Oft time after pleasance,
Trouble and grievance
370   No man can be sure
Alway to have pleasure:
As well perceive ye may
How my disport and play
From me was taken away
By Gib, our cat savage,
That in a furious rage
Caught Philip by the head
And slew him there stark dead.
        Kyrie, eleison,
380   *Christe, eleison,*
        Kyrie, eleison!
For Philip Sparrow's soul,
Set in our bead-roll,
Let us now whisper
A *Paternoster.*
        Lauda, anima mea, Dominum!
To weep with me look that ye come,
All manner of birds in your kind;
See none be left behind.
390   To mourning look that ye fall
With dolorous songs funeral,
Some to sing, and some to say,

Some to weep, and some to pray,
Every bird in his lay.
The goldfinch, the wagtail,
The jangling jay to rail,
The flecked pie to chatter
Of this dolorous matter;
And robin redbreast,
He shall be the priest
The requiem mass to sing,
Softly warbling,
With help of the reed sparrow,
And the chattering swallow,
The hearse for to hallow;
The lark with his long toe,
The spink, and the martinet also;
The shoveller with his broad beak,
The dotterel, that foolish peke,
And also the mad coot,
With bald face to toot;
The fieldfare and the snite,
The crow and the kite,
The raven, called Rolf,
His plain-song to sol-fa;
The partridge, the quail,
The plover with us to wail,
The woodhack, that singeth 'chur'
Hoarsely, as he had the mur,
The lusty chanting nightingale,
The popingay to tell her tale,
That tooteth oft in a glass,
Shall read the Gospel at mass;
The mavis with her whistle
Shall read there the Epistle.
    But with a large and a long
To keep just plain-song,
Our chanters shall be the cuckoo,
The culver, the stockdove,

With 'peewit' the lapwing,
        The Versicles shall sing.
            The bittern with his bump,
        The crane with his trump,
        The swan of Menander,
        The goose and the gander,
        The duck and the drake,
        Shall watch at this wake;
        The peacock so proud,
        Because his voice is loud,
440   And hath a glorious tail,
        He shall sing the Grail;
        The owl, that is so foul,
        Must help us to howl;
        The heron so gaunt,
        And the cormorant,
        With the pheasant,
        And the gaggling gant,
        And the churlish chough,
        The knot and the ruff,
450   The barnacle, the buzzard,
        With the wild mallard;
        The divendop to sleep,
        The waterhen to weep;
        The puffin and the teal,
        Money they shall deal
        To poor folk at large,
        That shall be their charge;
        The seamew and the titmouse,
        The woodcock with her long nose,
460   The throstle with her warbling,
        The starling with her brabbling,
        The rook, with the osprey
        That putteth fishes to a fray;
        And the dainty curlew,
        With the turtle most true.
            At this *Placebo*

We may not well forgo
The countering of the coe;
The stork also,
470 That maketh his nest
In chimneys to rest:
Within those walls
No broken galls
May there abide
Of cuckoldry side,
Or else philosophy
Maketh a great lie.
        The ostrich, that will eat
An horseshoe so great,
480 In the stead of meat,
Such fervent heat
His stomach doth frete:
He cannot well fly,
Nor sing tunably,
Yet at a brayd
He hath well assayed
To sol-fa above E-la:
Fa, lorell, fa, fa!
Ne quando
490 *Male cantando;*
The best that we can,
To make him our bell-man,
And let him ring the bells.
He can do nothing else.
        Chanticleer, our cock,
Must tell what is of the clock
By the astrology
That he hath naturally
Conceived and caught,
500 And was never taught
By Albumazer
The astronomer,
Nor by Ptolomy

52

Prince of astronomy,
Nor yet by Haly;
And yet he croweth daily
And nightly the tides
That no man abides,
With Partlot his hen,
510 Whom now and then
He plucketh by the head
When he doth her tread.

    The bird of Araby,
That potentially
May never die,
And yet there is none
But one alone:
A phoenix it is
This hearse that must bless
520 With aromatic gums
That cost great sums,
The way of thurification
To make a fumigation,
Sweet of reflare,
And redolent of air,
This corse for to cense
With great reverence,
As patriarch or pope
In a black cope.
530 Whiles he censeth the hearse,
He shall sing the verse,
Libe ra me,
In de, la, sol, re,
Softly bemole
For my sparrow's soul.
Pliny showeth all
In his *Story Natural*
What he doth find
Of the phoenix kind;
540 Of whose incineration

There riseth a new creation
Of the same fashion
Without alteration,
Saving that old age
Is turned unto courage
Of fresh youth again;
This matter true and plain,
Plain matter indeed,
Whoso list to read
550   But for the eagle doth fly
Highest in the sky,
He shall be the sedean,
The choir to demean,
As provost principal,
To teach them their Ordinal;
Also the noble falcon,
With the ger-falcon,
The tercel genteel,
They shall mourn soft and still
560   In their amice of grey;
The sacre with them shall say
Dirige for Philip's soul;
The goshawk shall have a roll
The choristers to control;
The lanners and merlins
Shall stand in their mourning gowns;
The hobby and the musket
The censers and the cross shall fet;
The kestrel in all this work
570   Shall be holy water clerk.
    And now the dark cloudy night
Chaseth away Phoebus bright,
Taking his course toward the west,
God send my sparrow's soul good rest!
    Requiem aeternam dona eis, Domine.
Fa, fa, fa, mi, re,
    A por ta in feri,

Fa, fa, fa, mi, mi.
Credo videre bona Domini,
580 I pray God, Philip to heaven may fly;
Domine, exaudi orationem meam!

To heaven he shall, from heaven he came;
Do mi nus vo bis cum,
Of all good prayers God send him some!
Oremus:
Deus, cui proprium est misereri et parcere,
On Philip's soul have pity!
For he was a pretty cock,
And came of a gentle stock,
590 And wrapped in a maiden's smock,
And cherished full daintily,
Till cruel fate made him to die:
Alas, for doleful destiny!
But whereto should I
Longer mourn or cry?
To Jupiter I call,
Of heaven imperial,
That Philip may fly
Above the starry sky,
600 To tread the pretty wren,
That is our Lady's hen.
Amen, amen, amen!
Yet one thing is behind,
That now cometh to mind:
An epitaph I would have
For Philip's grave.
But for I am a maid,
Timorous, half afraid,
That never yet assayed
610 Of Helicon's well,
Where the Muses dwell;
Though I can read and spell,
Recount, report, and tell
Of the *Tales of Canterbury,*

Some sad stories, some merry,
As Palamon and Arcet,
Duke Theseus, and Partelet,
And of the Wife of Bath,
That worketh much scath
620   When her tale is told
Among housewives bold,
How she controlled
Her husbands as she would,
And them to despise
In the homeliest wise,
Bring other wives in thought
Their husbands to set at nought.
And though that read have I
Of Gawain and Sir Guy,
630   And tell can a great piece
Of the Golden Fleece,
How Jason it won,
Like a valiant man;
Of Arthur's Round Table,
With his knights commendable,
And Dame Gaynor, his queen,
Was somewhat wanton, I ween;
How Sir Lancelot de Lake
Many a spear brake
640   For his lady's sake;
Of Tristram and King Mark
And all the whole work
Of Belle Isold his wife,
For whom was much strife;
Some say she was light,
And made her husband knight
Of the common hall,
That cuckolds men call;
And Sir Lybius,
650   Named Dysconius;
Of *Quater Fylz Amund*,

And how they were summoned
To Rome, to Charlemagne,
Upon a great pain,
And how they rode each one
On Bayard Mountalbon—
Men see him now and then
In the forest of Arden.
What though I can frame
660 The stories by name
Of Judas Maccabeus,
And of Caesar Julius,
And of the love between
Paris and Vienne,
And of the duke Hannibal,
That made the Romans all
Fordread and to quake;
How Scipion did wake
The city of Carthage,
670 Which by his merciful rage
He beat down to the ground.
And though I can expound
Of Hector of Troy,
That was all their joy,
Whom Achilles slew,
Wherefore all Troy did rue;
And of the love so hot
That made Troilus to dote
Upon fair Cresseid;
680 And what they wrote and said,
And of their wanton wills
Pandar bare the bills
From one to the other,
His master's love to further;
Sometime a precious thing,
An ouche or else a ring,
From her to him again;
Sometime a pretty chain,

Or a bracelet of her hair,
690 Prayed Troilus for to wear
That token for her sake:
How heartily he did it take,
And much thereof did make;
And all that was in vain,
For she did but feign.
The story telleth plain,
He could not obtain,
Though his father were a king.
Yet there was a thing
700 That made the male to wring:
She made him to sing
The song of lover's lay;
Musing night and day,
Mourning all alone,
Comfort had he none,
For she was quite gone.
Thus, in conclusion,
She brought him in abusion;
In earnest and in game
710 She was much to blame;
Disparaged is her fame.
And blemished is her name,
In manner half with shame;
Troilus also hath lost
On her much love and cost,
And now must kiss the post;
Pandar, that went between,
Hath won nothing, I ween,
But light for summer green;
720 Yet for a special laud
He is named Troilus' bawd;
Of that name he is sure
Whiles the world shall dure.

Though I remember the fable
Of Penelope most stable,

To her husband most true,
Yet long time she ne knew
Whether he were alive or dead;
Her wit stood her in stead,
730 That she was true and just
For any bodily lust
To Ulysses her make,
And never would him forsake.
  Of Marcus Marcellus
A process I could tell us;
And of Antiochus,
And of Josephus'
De Antiquitatibus,
And of Mardocheus,
740 And of great Ahasuerus,
And of Vesca his queen,
Whom he forsook with teen,
And of Esther his other wife,
With whom he led a pleasant life;
Of King Alexander,
And of King Evander,
And of Porsena the great,
That made the Romans to sweat.
  Though I have enrolled
750 A thousand new and old
Of these historious tales,
To fill budgets and males
With books that I have read,
Yet I am nothing sped,
And can but little skill
Of Ovid or Virgil,
Or of Plutarch,
Or Francis Petrarch,
Alcaeus or Sappho,
760 Or such other poets mo,
As Linus and Homerus,
Euphorion and Theocritus,

Anacreon and Arion,
Sophocles and Philemon,
Pindarus and Simonides,
Philistion and Pherecydes;
These poets of ancient,
They are too diffuse for me.
    For, as I tofore have said,
770   I am but a young maid,
And cannot in effect
My style as yet direct
With English words elect.
Our natural tongue is rude,
And hard to be ennewed
With polished terms lusty;
Our language is so rusty,
So cankered and so full
Of frowards, and so dull,
780   That if I would apply
To write ornately
I wot not where to find
Terms to serve my mind.
    Gower's English is old,
And of no value told:
His matter is worth gold,
And worthy to be enrolled.
    In Chaucer I am sped,
His tales I have read:
790   His matter is delectable,
Solacious, and commendable;
His English well allowed,
So as it is enprowed,
For as it is employed,
There is no English void,
At those days much commended;
And now men would have amended
His English, whereat they bark,
And mar all they work.

800 Chaucer, that famous clerk,
   His terms were not dark,
   But pleasant, easy, and plain;
   No word he wrote in vain.
    Also John Lydgate
   Writeth after an higher rate;
   It is diffuse to find
   The sentence of his mind,
   Yet writeth he in his kind,
   No man that can amend
810 Those matters that he hath penned;
   Yet some men find a fault,
   And say he writeth too haut.
    Wherefore hold me excused
   If I have not well perused
   Mine English half abused;
   Though it be refused,
   In worth I shall it take,
   And fewer words make.
    But, for my sparrow's sake,
820 Yet as a woman may,
   My wit I shall assay
   An epitaph to write
   In Latin plain and light,
   Whereof the elegy
   Followeth by and by:
   Flos volucrum formose, vale!
   Philippe, sub isto
   Marmore jam recubas,
   Qui mihi carus eras.
830 *Semper erunt nitido*
   Radiantia sidera coelo;
   Impressusque meo
   Pectore semper eris.
    Per me laurigerum
   Britonum Skeltonida Vatem
   Haec cecinisse licet

Ficta sub imagine texta.
Cujus eris volucris,
Praestanti corpore virgo:
840 *Candida Nais erat,*
Formosior ista Joanna est:
Docta Corinna fuit,
Sed magis ista sapit.
    Bien m'en souvient.

    The Commendations.
    Beati immaculati in via,
       O gloriosa femina!
Now mine whole imagination
And studious meditation
Is to take this commendation
850 In this consideration;
And under patient toleration
Of that most goodly maid
That *Placebo* hath said,
And for her sparrow prayed
In lamentable wise,
Now will I enterprise,
Through the grace divine
Of the Muses nine,
Her beauty to commend,
860 If Arethusa will send
Me influence to indite,
And with my pen to write;
If Apollo will promise
Melodiously it to devise
His tunable harp strings
With harmony that sings
Of princes and kings
And of all pleasant things,
Of lust and of delight,
870 Through his godly might;
To whom be the laud ascribed

62

That my pen hath imbibed
With the aureate drops,
As verily my hope is,
Of Tagus, that golden flood,
That passeth all earthly good;
And as that flood doth pass
All floods that ever was
With his golden sands,
880 Whoso that understands
Cosmography, and the streams,
And the floods in strange reams,
Right so she doth exceed
All other of whom we read,
Whose fame by me shall spread
Into Persia and Mede,
From Britain's Albion
To the Tower of Babylon.
  I trust it is no shame,
890 And no man will me blame,
Though I register her name
In the court of Fame;
For this most goodly flower,
This blossom of fresh colour,
So Jupiter me succour,
She flourisheth new and new
In beauty and virtue:
Hac claritate gemina,
O gloriosa femina,
900 *Retribue servo tuo, vivifica me!*
Labia mea laudabunt te.
  But enforced am I
Openly to ascry,
And to make an outcry
Against odious Envy,
That evermore will lie,
And say cursedly—
With his leather eye,

And cheeks dry;
910   With visage wan,
As swart as tan;
His bones creak,
Lean as a rake;
His gums rusty
Are full unlusty;
His heart withal
Bitter as gall;
His liver, his lung
With anger is wrung;
920   His serpent's tongue
That many one hath stung;
He frowneth ever,
He laugheth never,
Even nor morrow,
But other men's sorrow
Causeth him to grin
And rejoice therein;
No sleep can him catch,
But ever doth watch;
930   He is so beat
With malice, and frete
With anger and ire,
His foul desire
Will suffer no sleep
In his head to creep;
His foul semblant
All displeasant;
When other are glad,
Then is he sad
940   Frantic and mad;
His tongue never still
For to say ill,
Writhing and wringing,
Biting and stinging;
And thus this elf

Consumeth himself,
Himself doth slo
With pain and woe—
This false Envy
950 Saith that I
Use great folly
For to indite,
And for to write,
And spend my time
In prose and rhyme,
For to express
The nobleness
Of my mistress,
That causeth me
960 Studious to be
To make a relation
Of her commendation.
And there again
Envy doth complain,
And hath disdain;
But yet certain
I will be plain,
And my style dress
To this process.
970   Now Phoebus me ken
To sharp my pen,
And lead my fist
As him best list,
That I may say
Honour alway
Of womankind.
Truth doth me bind,
And loyalty,
Ever to be
980 Their true beadle,
To write and tell
How women excel

In nobleness;
As my mistress,
Of whom I think
With pen and ink
For to compile
Some goodly style;
For this most goodly flower,
990 This blossom of fresh colour,
So Jupiter me succour,
She flourisheth new and new
In beauty and virtue:
Hac claritate gemina,
O gloriosa femina,
Legem pone mihi domina, viam justificationem tuarum!
Quemadmodum desiderat cervus ad fontes aquarum.
 How shall I report
All the goodly sort
1000 Of her features clear,
That hath none earthly peer?
Her favour of her face
Ennewed all with grace,
Comfort, pleasure and solace.
Mine heart doth so embrace,
And so hath ravished me,
Her to behold and see,
That in words plain
I cannot me refrain
1010 To look on her again.
Alas, what should I feign?
It were a pleasant pain
With her aye to remain.
 Her eyen grey and steep
Causeth mine heart to leap;
With her brows bent
She may well represent
Fair Lucrece, as I ween,
Or else fair Polexene,

<pre>
1020   Or else Calliope,
        Or else Penelope;
        For this most goodly flower,
        This blossom of fresh colour,
        So Jupiter me succour,
        She flourisheth new and new
        In beauty and virtue:
        Hac claritate gemina,
        O gloriosa femina,
        Memor esto verbi tui servo tuo!
1030   *Servuus tuus sum ego.*
            The Indy sapphire blue
        Her veins doth ennew;
        The orient pearl so clear,
        The whiteness of her lere;
        Her lusty ruby ruddes
        Resemble the rose buds;
        Her lips soft and merry
        Enbloomed like the cherry:
        It were an heavenly bliss
1040   Her sugared mouth to kiss.
            Her Beauty to augment,
        Dame Nature hath her lent
        A wart upon her cheek,
        Whoso list to seek;
        In her visage a scar,
        That seemeth from afar
        Like to the radiant star,
        All with favour fret,
        So properly it is set.
1050   She is the violet,
        The daisy delectable,
        The columbine commendable,
        The jelofer amiable:
        This most goodly flower,
        This blossom of fresh colour,
        So Jupiter me succour,
</pre>

She flourisheth new and new
In beauty and virtue:
Hac claritate gemina,
1060   *O gloriosa femina,*
Bonitatem fecisti cum servo tuo, domina,
Et ex praecordiis sonant praeconia!
    And when I perceived
Her wart and conceived,
It cannot be denied
But it was well conveyed
And set so womanly,
And nothing wantonly,
But right conveniently,
1070   And full congruently,
As Nature could devise,
In most goodly wise.
Whose list behold,
It maketh lovers bold
To her to sue for grace,
Her favour to purchase;
The scar upon her chin,
Enhatched on her fair skin,
Whiter than the swan—
1080   It would make any man
To forget deadly sin
Her favour to win!
For this most goodly flower,
This blossom of fresh colour,
So Jupiter me succour,
She flourisheth new and new
In beauty and virtue:
Hac claritate gemina,
O gloriosa femina,
1090   *Defecit in salutatione tua anima mea;*
Quid petis filio, mater dulcissima? babae!
    Soft, and make no din,
For now I will begin

68

To have in remembrance
Her goodly dalliance,
And her goodly pastance:
So sad and demure,
Behaving her so sure,
With words of pleasure
1100   She would make to the lure,
And any man convert
To give her his whole heart.
She made me sore amazed
Upon her when I gazed:
Methought mine heart was crazed,
My eyen were so dazed,
For this most goodly flower,
This blossom of fresh colour,
So Jupiter me succour,
1110   She flourisheth new and new
In beauty and virtue:
Hac claritate gemina,
O gloriosa femina,
Quomodo dilexi legem tuam, domina!
Recedant vetera, nova sunt omnia.

And to amend her tale,
When she list to avail,
And with her fingers small,
And hands soft as silk,
1120   Whiter than milk,
That are so quickly veined,
Wherewith my hand she strained,
Lord, how I was pained!
Unneth me I refrained,
How she me had reclaimed,
And me to her retained,
Embracing therewithall
Her goodly middle small,
With sides long and straight.
1130   To tell you what conceit

I had then in a trice,
The matter were too nice:
And yet there was no vice,
Nor yet no villainy,
But only fantasy.
For this most goodly flower,
This blossom of fresh colour,
So Jupiter me succour,
She flourisheth new and new
1140 In beauty and virtue:
Hac claritate gemina,
O gloriosa femina,
Iniquos odio habui!
Non calumnientur me superbi.
    But whereto should I note
How often did I toot
Upon her pretty foot?
It razed mine heart root
To see her tread the ground
1150 With heels short and round.
She is plainly express
Egeria, the goddess,
And like to her image,
Emportured with courage,
A lover's pilgrimage;
There is no beast savage,
Ne no tiger so wood,
But she would change his mood:
Such relucent grace
1160 Is formed in her face.
For this most goodly flower,
This blossom of fresh colour,
So Jupiter me succour,
She flourisheth new and new
In beauty and virtue:
Hac claritate gemina,
O gloriosa femina,

Mirabilia testimonia tua!
Sicut novellae plantationes in juventute sua.

1170   So goodly as she dresses,
So properly she presses
The bright golden tresses
Of her hair so fine,
Like Phoebus' beams shine.
Whereto should I disclose
The gartering of her hose?
It is for to suppose
How that she can wear
Gorgeously her gear;

1180   Her fresh habiliments
With other implements
To serve for all intents,
Like Dame Flora, queen
Of lusty summer green.
This most goodly flower,
This blossom of fresh colour,
So Jupiter me succour,
She flourisheth new and new
In beauty and virtue:

1190   *Hac claritate gemina,*
O gloriosa femina,
Clamavi in toto corde, exaudi me!
Misericordia tua magna est super me.

Her kirtle so goodly laced,
And under that is braced
Such pleasures that I may
Neither write nor say.
Yet though I write not with ink,
No man can let me think,

1200   For thought hath liberty,
Thought is frank and free;
To think a merry thought
It cost me little or nought.
Would God mine homely style

71

Were polished with the file
Of Cicero's eloquence,
To praise her excellence.
For this most goodly flower,
This blossom of fresh colour,
1210   So Jupiter me succour,
She flourisheth new and new
In beauty and virtue:
Hac claritate gemina,
O gloriosa femina,
Principes persecuti sunt me gratis!
Omnibus consideratis,
Paradisus voluptatis
Haec virgo est dulcissima.

    My pen it is unable,
1220   My hand it is unstable,
My reason rude and dull
To praise her at the full;
Goodly Mistress Jane,
Sober, demure Diane;
Jane this mistress hight,
The lode-star of delight,
Dame Venus of all pleasure,
The well of worldly treasure;
She doth exceed and pass
1230   In prudence Dame Pallas.
This most goodly flower,
This blossom of fresh colour,
So Jupiter me succour,
She flourisheth new and new
In beauty and virtue:
Hac claritate gemina,
O gloriosa femina!

    Requiem aeternam dona eis, Domine.
With this psalm, *Domine, probasti me,*
1240   Shall sail over the sea,
With *tibi, Domine, commendamus,*

On pilgrimage to Saint James,
For shrimps and for prawns,
And for stalking cranes.
And where my pen hath offended,
I pray you it may be amended
By discreet consideration
Of your wise reformation:
I have not offended, I trust,
1250   If it be sadly discussed.
It were no gentle guise
This treatise to despise,
Because I have written and said
Honour of this fair maid.
Wherefore should I be blamed
That I Jane have named
And famously proclaimed?
She is worthy to be enrolled
With letters of gold.
       Car elle vaut.

THE TUNNING OF ELINOUR RUMMING

Tell you I chill,
If that ye will
Awhile be still,
Of a comely gill
That dwelt on a hill:
But she is not gryll,
For she is somewhat sage
And well worn in age,
For her visage
10   It would assuage
A man's courage.
    Her loathly lere
Is nothing clear,
But ugly of cheer,

Droopy and drowsy,
Scurvy and lousy;
Her face all boozy,
Comely crinkled,
Wondrously wrinkled,
Like a roast pig's ear,
Bristled with hair.
 Her lewd lips twain,
They slaver, men sayne,
Like a ropy rain,
A gummy glayre.
She is ugly fair:
Her nose somedele hooked,
And camously crooked,
Never stopping,
But ever dropping;
Her skin loose and slack,
Grained like a sack;
With a crooked back.
 Her eyen gowndy
Are full unsoundy,
For they are bleared;
And she grey haired,
Jawed like a jetty;
A man would have pity
To see how she is gummed,
Fingered and thumbed,
Gently jointed,
Greased and anointed
Up to the knuckles;
The bones of her huckles
Like as they were with buckles
Together made fast—
Her youth is far past.
Footed like a plane,
Legged like a crane,
And yet she will jet

74

Like a jolly fet,
In her furred flocket,
And grey russet rocket,
With simper-the-cocket.
Her huke of Lincoln green
It had been hers, I ween,
More than forty year,
And so doth it appear,
60   For the green bare threads
Look like sere weeds,
Withered like hay,
The wool worn away.
And yet I dare say
She thinketh herself gay
Upon the holy day,
When she doth her array,
And girdeth in her gites,
Stitched and pranked with pleats;
70   Her kirtle Bristol-red,
With clothes upon her head
That weigh a sow of lead,
Writhen in wonder wise
After the Saracen's guise,
With a whim-wham
Knit with a trim-tram
Upon her brain-pan,
Like an Egyptian
Lapped about.
80   When she goeth out
Herself for to show,
She driveth down the dew
With a pair of heels
As broad as two wheels;
She hobbles as she goes
With her blanket hose
Over the fallow;
Her shoon smeared with tallow,

Greased upon dirt
90 That baudeth her skirt.

   Primus Passus
  And this comely dame,
I understand her name
Is Elinour Rumming,
At home in her wonning;
And as men say
She dwelt in Surrey,
In a certain stead
Beside Leatherhead.
She is a tunnish gib;
100 The devil and she be sib.
  But to make up my tale,
She breweth nappy ale,
And maketh thereof port-sale
To travellers, to tinkers,
To sweaters, to swinkers,
And all good ale drinkers,
That will nothing spare,
But drink till they stare
And bring themselves bare,
110 With, 'now away the mare,
And let us slay care!'
As wise as an hare!
  Come whoso will
To Elinour on the hill
With, 'fill the cup, fill!'
And sit there by still,
Early and late.
Thither cometh Kate,
Cicely and Sarah,
120 With their legs bare,
And also their feet
Hardly full unsweet;
With their heels dagged,

Their kirtles all to-jagged,
Their smocks all to-ragged,
With titters and tatters,
Bring dishes and platters,
With all their might running
To Elinour Rumming
130   To have of her tunning;
She loaneth them on the same,
And thus beginneth the game.
    Some wenches come unlaced,
Some housewives come unbraced,
With their naked paps
That flips and flaps,
It wigs and it wags
Like tawny saffron bags—
A sort of foul drabs
140   All scurvy with scabs.
Some be flybitten,
Some skewed as a kitten;
Some with a shoe clout
Bind their heads about;
Some have no hair-lace,
Their locks about their face,
Their tresses untrussed
All full of unlust;
Some look strawry,
150   Some cawry-mawry:
Full untidy teggs,
Like rotten eggs:
Such a lewd sort
To Elinour resort
From tide to tide.
Abide, abide,
And to you shall be told
How her ale is sold
To malt and to mould.

160   Some have no money
  That thither commy
  For their ale to pay—
  That is a shrewd array!
  Elinour sweared, 'nay,
  Ye shall not bear away
  Mine ale for nought,
  By Him that me bought!'
  With, 'hey, dog, hey,
  Have these hogs away!'

170 With, 'get me a staff,
  The swine eat my draff!
  Strike the hogs with a club,
  They have drunk up my swilling-tub!'
  For, be there never so much press,
  These swine go to the high dais,
  The sow with her pigs,
  The boar his tail wrigs,
  His rump also he frigs
  Against the high bench:

180 With, 'fo, there is a stench!
  Gather up, thou wench;
  Seest thou not what is fall?
  Take up dirt and all,
  And bear out of the hall.'
  God give it ill-preving,
  Cleanly as evil 'chieving!
   But let us turn plain,
  There we left again.
  For as ill a patch as that,

190 The hens run in the mash-vat;
  For they go to roost
  Straight over the ale-joust,
  And dung, when it comes,
  In the ale-tuns.
  Then Elinour taketh

The mash-bowl, and shaketh
The hens' dung away,
And skimmeth it into a tray
Whereas the yeast is,
200   With her mangy fists;
And sometimes she blends
The dung of her hens
And the ale together,
And sayeth, 'gossip, come hither,
The ale shall be thicker;
And flower the more quicker;
For I may tell you
I learned it of a jew
When I began to brew,
210   And I have found it true.
Drink now while it is new,
And ye may it brook:
It shall make you look
Younger than ye be
Years two or three,
For ye may prove it by me.'
'Behold,' she said, 'and see
How bright I am of ble!
Ich am not cast away,
220   That can my husband say,
When we kiss and play
In lust and in liking;
He calleth me his whiting,
His mulling and his miting,
His nobbes and his coney,
His sweeting and his honey,
With, 'buss, my pretty bonny,
Thou art worth good and money.'
Thus make I my falyre fonny,
230   Till that he dream and drony;
For after all our sport,
Then will he rout and snort;

Thus sweet together we lie
As two pigs in a sty.'
   To cease meseemeth best,
And of this tale to rest,
And for to leave this letter
Because it is no better;
And because it is no sweeter,
240 We will no further rhyme
Of it at this time,
But we will turn plain
Where we left again.

   Tertius Passus
   Instead of coin and money
Some bring her a coney,
And some a pot with honey,
Some a salt, and some a spoon,
Some their hose, some their shoon;
Some ran a good trot
250 With a skillet or a pot;
Some fill their pot full
Of good Lemster wool:
An housewife of trust,
When she is athirst,
Such a web can spin,
Her thrift is full thin.
   Some go straight thither,
Be it slaty or slither;
They hold the highway,
260 They care not what men say.
Be that as be may,
Some loth to be espied,
Some start in at the back-side,
Over the hedge and pale,
And all for the good ale.
   Some run till they sweat,
Bring with them malt or wheat,

And Dame Elinour entreat
To birle them of the best.
270   Then cometh another guest:
She sweareth by the rood of rest
Her lips are so dry
Without drink she must die,
Therefore fill it by and by,
And have here a peck of rye.
        Anon cometh another,
As dry as the other,
And with her doth bring
Meat, salt, or other thing,
280   Her harvest girdle, her wedding-ring,
To pay for her scot
As cometh to her lot.
Some bringeth her husband's hood
Because the ale is good;
Another brought her his cap
To offer to the ale-tap,
With flax and with tow;
And some brought sour dough
With 'hey' and with 'ho,
290   Sit we down a row,
And drink till we blow,
And pipe tirly tirlow!'
        Some laid to pledge
Their hatchet and their wedge,
Their heckle and their reel,
Their rock, their spinning-wheel;
And some went so narrow
They laid to pledge their wharrow,
Their ribskin and their spindle,
300   Their needle and their thimble—
Here was scant thrift
When they made such a shift.
        Their thirst was so great
They asked never for meat,

But, 'drink, still drink,
And let the cat wink!
Let us wash our gums
From the dry crumbs!'

Quartus Passus
Some for very need
310   Laid down a skein of thread,
And some a skein of yarn;
Some brought from the barn
Both beans and peas—
Small chaffer doth ease
Sometime, now and then.
Another there was that ran
With a good brass-pan—
Her colour was full wan;
She ran in all the haste,
320   Unbraced and unlaced;
Tawny, swart, and sallow
Like a cake of tallow.
I swear by all hallow
It was a stale to take
The devil in a brake!
And then came halting Joan,
And brought a gambone
Of bacon that was resty;
But, Lord, as she was testy,
330   Angry as a waspy!
She began to yawn and gaspy,
And bade Elinour go bet
And fill in good met—
It was dear that was far-fet.
Another brought a spick
Of a bacon-flick;
Her tongue was very quick,
But she spake somewhat thick.
Her fellow did stammer and stut,

340   But she was a foul slut,
For her mouth foamed
And her belly groaned:
Joan said she had eaten a fyest.
'By Christ,' said she, 'thou liest;
I have as sweet a breath
As thou, with shameful death!'
    Then Elinour said, 'ye callets,
I shall break your palates,
Without ye now cease!'
350   And so was made the peace.
    Then hither came drunken Alice,
And she was full of tales,
Of tidings in Wales,
And of Saint James in Gales,
And of the Portingales,
With, 'lo, gossip, ywis,
Thus and thus it is:
There hath been great war
Between Temple Bar
360   And the Cross in Cheap,
And thither came an heap
Of mill-stones in a rout.'
She spake this in her snout,
Snivelling in her nose
As though she had the pose:
'Lo, here is an old tippet,
And ye will give me a sippet
Of your stale ale,
God send you good sale!'
370   And as she was drinking
She fell in a winking
With a barley-hood—
She pissed where she stood.
Then began she to weep,
And forthwith fell on sleep.
Elinour took her up

And blessed her with a cup
Of new ale in corns:
Alice found therein no thorns,
380   But supped it up at once—
She found therein no bones.

    Quintus Passus
    Now in cometh another rabble:
First one with a ladle,
Another with a cradle,
And with a side-saddle;
And there began a fable,
A clattering and a babble
Of a fool's filly
That had a foal with Willy,
390   With, 'jast, you,' and 'gup, gilly,
She could not lie stilly!'
Then came in a jennet
And swore, 'by Saint Bennet,
I drank not this sennight
A draught to my pay!
Elinour, I thee pray,
Of thine ale let us essay,
And have here a pilch of grey:
I wear skins of coney,
400   That causeth I look so dunny,'
Another then did hitch her,
And brought a pottle-pitcher,
A tunnel and a bottle,
But she had lost the stopple—
She cut off her shoe sole,
And stopped therewith the hole.
    Among all the blommer,
Another brought a skommer,
A frying-pan, and a slice;
410   Elinour made the price
For good ale each whit.

Then start in mad Kit
That had little wit:
She seemed somedele sick
And brought a penny chick
To Dame Elinour
For a draught of her liquor.
   Then Margery Milkduck
Her kirtle she did uptuck
An inch above her knee,
Her legs that ye might see;
But they were sturdy and stubbed,
Mighty pestles and clubbed,
As fair and as white
As the foot of a kite.
She was somewhat foul,
Crook-nebbed like an owl;
And yet she brought her fees:
A cantle of Essex cheese
Was well a foot thick,
Full of maggots quick:
It was huge and great,
And mighty strong meat
For the devil to eat—
It was tart and pungete.
Another sort of sluts:
Some brought walnuts,
Some apples, some pears,
Some brought their clipping shears,
Some brought this and that,
Some brought I wot ne'er what;
Some brought their husband's hat,
Some puddings and links,
Some tripes that stinks.
   But of all this throng
One came them among,
She seemed half a leech
And began to preach

Of the Tuesday in the week
450   When the mare doth kick;
Of the virtue of an unset leek;
Of her husband's breek;
With the feathers of a quail
She could to Bordeaux sail;
And with good ale barm
She could make a charm
To help withal a stitch—
She seemed to be a witch.
Another brought two goslings
460   That were noughty frostlings;
She brought them in a wallet—
She was a comely callet:
The goslings were untied;
Elinour began to chide,
'They be wretchocks thou hast brought,
They are sheer shaking nought!'

Sextus Passus
Maud Ruggy hither skipped:
She was ugly hipped,
And ugly thick lipped,
470   Like an onion sided,
Like tan leather hided.
She had her so guided
Between the cup and the wall
That she was there withal
Into a palsy fall;
With that her head shaked,
And her hands quaked—
One's head would have ached
To see her naked.
480   She drank so of the dregs;
The dropsy was in her legs;
Her face glistering like glass,
All foggy fat she was.

She had also the gout
In all her joints about;
Her breath was sour and stale,
And smelled all of ale—
Such a bedfellow
Would make one cast his craw.
490   But yet for all that
She drank on the mash-vat.

    There came an old ribibe:
She halted of a kibe,
And had broken her shin
At the threshold coming in,
And fell so wide open
That one might see her token—
The devil thereon be wroken!
What need all this be spoken?
500   She yelled like a calf.
'Rise up, on God's half!'
Said Elinour Rumming,
'I beshrew thee for thy coming!'
And as she at her did pluck,
'Quack, quack,' said the duck
In that lampatram's lap;
With, 'fie, cover thy shap
With some flip-flap!
God give it ill hap,'
510   Said Elinour, 'for shame—
Like an honest dame.'
Up she start, half lame,
And scantly could go
For pain and for woe.

    In came another dant,
With a goose and a gannet:
She had a wide weasant;
She was nothing pleasant:
Necked like an elephant;
520   It was a bulliphant,

87

A greedy cormorant.
Another brought her garlic heads,
Another brought her beads
Of jet or of coal
To offer to the ale-pole.
Some brought a wimble,
Some brought a thimble,
Some brought a silk lace,
Some brought a pincase,
530   Some her husband's gown,
Some a pillow of down,
Some of the napery;
And all this shift they make
For the good ale sake.
    'A straw!' said Bele, 'stand utter,
For we have eggs and butter,
And of pigeons a pair.'
    Then start forth a fizgig,
And she brought a boar pig;
540   The flesh thereof was rank,
And her breath strongly stank;
Yet, ere she went, she drank,
And got her great thank
Of Elinour for her ware
That she thither bare
To pay for her share.
Now truly to my thinking,
This is a solemn drinking!

    Septimus Passus
    'Soft!' quoth one hight Sybil,
550   'And let me with you bibble.'
She sat down in the place
With a sorry face
Whey-wormed about.
Garnished was her snout
With here and there a puscule

Like a scabbed mussel.
'This ale,' said she, 'is noppy;
Let us sup and soppy
And not spill a droppy,
560 For, so mote I hoppy,
It cooleth well my croppy.'
 'Dame Elinour,' said she,
'Have here is for me,
A clout of London pins.'
And with that she begins
The pot to her pluck,
And drank a good-luck.
She swinged up a quart
At once for her part:
570 Her paunch was so puffed,
And so with ale stuffed,
Had she not hied apace
She had defiled the place.
 Then began the sport
Among that drunken sort.
'Dame Elinour,' said they,
'Lend here a cock of hay
To make all thing clean—
Ye wot well what we mean!'
580 But, sir, among all
That sat in that hall
There was a prick-me-dainty
Sat like a sainty
And began to painty
As though she would fainty:
She made it as coy
As a lege moy;
She was not half so wise
As she was peevish nice.
590 She said never a word,
But rose from the board
And called for our dame
Elinour by name.

We supposed, ywis,
That she rose to piss:
But the very ground
Was for to compound
With Elinour in the spence,
To pay for her expense.

600 'I have no penny or groat
To pay,' said she, 'God wote,
For washing of my throat,
But my beads of amber;
Bear them to your chamber.'

Then Elinour did them hide
Within her bed's side.
But some then sat right sad
That nothing had
There of their own,

610 Neither gelt nor pawn:
Such were there many
That had not a penny.
But, when they should walk,
Were fain with a chalk
To score on the balk,
Or score on the tail:
God give it ill hail!
For my fingers itch—
I have written too much

620 Of this mad mumming
Of Elinour Rumming.
Thus endeth the geste
Of this worthy feast.

Quoth Skelton Laureat.

90

My name is Parrot, a bird of Paradise,
By nature devised of a wondrous kind,
Daintily dieted with divers delicate spice,
Till Euphrates, that flood, driveth me into Ind;
Where men of that country by fortune me find,
And send me to great ladies of estate;
Then Parrot must have an almond or a date.

A cage curiously carven, with silver pin,
Properly painted, to be my coverture;
10   A mirror of glass, that I may toot therein;
These maidens full merrily with many a divers flower,
Freshly they dress and make sweet my bower,
With 'speak, Parrot, I pray you,' full courteously they say,
'Parrot is a goodly bird and a pretty popagay.'

With my beak bent, my little wanton eye,
My feathers fresh as is the emerald green,
About my neck a circulet like the rich ruby,
My little legs, my feet both feat and clean,
I am a minion to wait upon a queen;
20   'My proper Parrot, my little pretty fool'—
With ladies I learn, and go with them to school.

'He, ha, ha, Parrot, ye can laugh prettily!'
Parrot hath not dined of all this long day.
Like our puss-cat Parrot can mewte and cry
In Latin, in Hebrew, and in Chaldee;
In Greek tongue Parrot can both speak and say,
As Persius, that poet, doth report of me,
'*Quis expedivit psittaco suum chaire?*'

Douce French of Paris Parrot can learn,
30   Pronouncing my purpose after my property,
With '*parlez bien*, Parrot, *ou parlez rien*.'

91

With Dutch, with Spanish, my tongue can agree,
In English to God Parrot can supplee:
'Christ save King Henry the Eighth, our royal king,
The red rose in honour to flourish and spring!

With Katherine incomparable, our royal queen also,
That peerless pomegranate, Christ save her noble grace!'
Parrot *saves habler Castiliano*,
With *fidasso de cosso* in Turkey and in Thrace;
40   *Vis consilii expers*, as teacheth me Horace,
Mole ruit sua, whose dictes are pregnant—
Soventez foys, Parrot, *en souvenaunte*.

My lady mistress, Dame Philology,
Gave me a gift, in my nest when I lay,
To learn all language, and it to speak aptly.
Now *pandez mory*, wax frantic, some men say;
Phronesis for phrenesis may not hold her way.
An almond now for Parrot, delicately dressed—
In *salve festa dies, toto* is the best.

50   *Moderata juvant*, but *toto* doth exceed;
Discretion is mother of noble virtues all;
Myden agen in Greeks' tongue we read,
But reason and wit wanteth their provincial
When wilfulness is vicar general.
Haec res acu tangitur, Parrot, *par ma foy*—
Tycez-vous, Parrot, *tenes-vous coye*.

Busy, busy, busy, and business again!
'*Que pensez-vous*, Parrot? what meaneth this business?'
Vitulus in Horeb troubled Aaron's brain,
60   Melchizedek merciful made Moloch merciless.
Too wise is no virtue, too meddling, too restless;
In measure is treasure, *cum sensu maturato*,
Ne tropo sanno, ne tropo mato.

Aram was fired with Chaldee's fire called Ur;
Jobab was brought up in the land of Hus;
The lineage of Lot took support of Assur;
Jereboseth is Hebrew, who list the cause discuss—
'Peace, Parrot, ye prate as ye were *ebrius:*'
Howst thee, *lyver god van hemrik ic seg!*
70   In Popering grew pears when Parrot was an egg.

'What is this to purpose?' Over in a whinnymeg!
Hop Lobin of Lowdeon would have a bit of bread;
The gibbet of Baldock was made for Jack Leg;
An arrow unfeathered and without an head,
A bagpipe without blowing standeth in no stead:
Some run too far before, some run too far behind,
Some be too churlish, and some be too kind.

Ic dien serveth for the ostrich feather,
Ic dien is the language of the land of Beme;
80   In Afric tongue *byrsa* is a thong of leather;
In Palestina there is Jerusalem.
Colustrum now for Parrot, white bread and sweet cream!
Our Thomasen she doth trip, our Jennet she doth shail—
Parrot hath a black beard and a fair green tail.

'Morish mine own shelf,' the costermonger saith,
Fate, fate, fate, ye Irish waterlag;
In flattering fables men find but little faith,
But *moveatur terra,* let the world wag;
Let Sir Wrig-wrag wrestle with Sir Dallyrag;
90   Every man after his manner of ways:
Pawbe une arver, so the Welshman says.

Such shreds of sentence, strewed in the shop
Of ancient Aristippus and such other more,
I gather together and close in my crop
Of my wanton conceit, *unde depromo
Dilemmata docta in paedagogio*

Sacro vatem, whereof to you I break—
I pray you, let Parrot have liberty to speak.

'But ware the cat, Parrot, ware the false cat!'
100 With, 'who is there—a maid?' Nay, nay, I trow!
'Ware riot, Parrot, ware riot, ware that!'
Meat, meat for Parrot, meat I say, ho!
Thus diverse of language by learning I grow,
With, 'buss me, sweet Parrot, buss me, sweet sweet,'
To dwell among ladies Parrot is meet.

'Parrot, Parrot, Parrot, pretty popagay!'
With my beak I can pick my little pretty toe;
My delight is solace, pleasure, disport, and play;
Like a wanton, when I will, I reel to and fro:
110 Parrot can say *Caesar ave!* also;
But Parrot hath no favour to Esebon:
Above all other birds set Parrot alone.

Ulula, Esebon, for Jeremy doth weep!
Zion is in sadness, Rachel ruely doth look;
Midionita Jethro, our Moses keepeth his sheep;
Gideon is gone, that Zalmane undertook,
Horeb *et* Zeb, of *Judicum* read the book.
Now Geball, Ammon, and Amaloch—'Hark, hark,
Parrot pretendeth to be a Bible clerk!'

120 O Esebon, Esebon, to thee is come again,
Sihon, the regent *Amorraeorum*,
And Og, that fat hog of Bashan, doth retain
The crafty *coistronus Cananaeorum*; .
And *asylum*, whilom *refugium miserorum,
Non fanum, sed profanum*, standeth in little stead—
Ulula, Esebon, for Jephtha is stark dead!

Esebon, Marybone, Whetstone next Barnet;
A trim-tram for an horse-mill it were a nice thing;

94

Dainties for damoiselles, chaffer far-fet;
130   Bo-ho doth bark well, but ho-ho he ruleth the ring;
From Scarpary to Tartary renown therein doth spring,
With, 'he said,' and, 'we said,' ich wot now what ich wot,
Quod magnus est dominus Judas Iscariot!

Ptolemy and Haly were cunning and wise
In the volvel, in the quadrant, and in the astrolaby,
To prognosticate truly the chance of Fortune's dice;
Some treat of their tyrkis, some of astrology,
Some *pseudo-propheta* with chiromancy.
If Fortune be friendly, and grace be the guide,
140   Honour with renown will run on that side.

          Monon colon agaton,
          Quoth Parrato
          In Graeco.

Let Parrot, I pray you, have liberty to prate,
For *aurea lingua Graeca* ought to be magnified,
If it were conned perfectly, and after the rate,
As *Lingua Latina*, in school matter occupied,
But our Greeks their Greek so well have applied
That they cannot say in Greek, riding by the way,
150   'Ho, hostler, fetch my horse a bottle of hay!'

Neither frame a syllogism in *phrisemorum*,
Formaliter et Graece, cum medio termino.
Our Greeks ye wallow in the wash-bowl *Argolicorum*;
For though ye can tell in Greek what is *phormio*,
Yet ye seek out your Greek in *Capricornio*;
For they scrape out good scripture, and set in a gall:
Ye go about to amend, and ye mar all.

Some argue *secundum quid ad simpliciter*,
And yet he would be reckoned *pro Areopagita*;
160   And some make distinctions *multiplicita*,

Whether *ita* were before *non*, or *non* before *ita*,
Neither wise nor well-learned, but like *hermaphrodita*.
Set *sophia* aside, for every Jack Raker
And every mad meddler must now be a maker.

In *Academia* Parrot dare no problem keep,
For *Graece fari* so occupieth the chair
That *Latinum fari* may fall to rest and sleep,
And *syllogisari* was drowned at Stourbridge Fair;
Trivials and quatrivials so sore now they appair
170 That Parrot the popagay hath pity to behold
How the rest of good learning is roufled up and trold.

Albertus de modo significandi,
And *Donatus* be driven out of school;
Priscian's head broken now handy-dandy,
And *Inter didascolos* is reckoned for a fool;
Alexander, a gander of Menander's pool,
With *De Causales* is cast out of the gate,
And *De Rationales* dare not show his pate.

Plautus in his comedies a child shall now rehearse,
180 And meddle with Quintilian in his *Declamations*,
That *Petty Cato* can scantly construe a verse,
With *Aveto in Graeco*, and such solemn salutations,
Can scantly the tenses of his conjugations;
Setting their minds so much of eloquence
That of their school matters lost is the whole sentence.

Now a nutmeg, a nutmeg, *cum garyophyllo*,
For Parrot to pick upon, his brain for to stable,
Sweet cinnamon sticks and *pleris cum musco*.
In Paradise, that place of pleasure perdurable,
190 The progeny of parrots were fair and favourable;
Now in *valle* Hebron Parrot is fain to feed—
'Christ-Cross and Saint Nicholas, Parrot, be your good speed!'

The mirror that I toot in, *quasi diaphanum,*
Vel quasi speculum, in aenigmate,
Elencticum, or else *enthymematicum,*
For logicians to look on, somewhat *sophistice;*
Rhetoricians and orators in fresh humanity,
Support Parrot, I pray you, with your suffrage ornate,
Of *confuse tantum* avoiding the checkmate.

200   But of this supposition that called is art,
Confuse distributive, as Parrot hath devised,
Let every man after his merit take his part;
For in this process Parrot nothing hath surmised,
No matter pretended, nor nothing enterprised,
But that *metaphora, allegoria* with all,
Shall be his protection, his paves, and his wall.

For Parrot is no churlish chough, nor no flecked pie,
Parrot is no pendugum, that men call a carling,
Parrot is no woodcock, nor no butterfly,
210   Parrot is no stammering stare, that men call a starling;
But Parrot is my own dear heart and my dear darling.
Melpomene, that fair maid, she burnished his beak—
I pray you, let Parrot have liberty to speak!

Parrot is a fair bird for a lady;
God of His goodness him framed and wrought;
When Parrot is dead she doth not putrefy;
Yea, all thing mortal shall turn unto nought,
Except man's soul, that Christ so dear bought;
220   That never may die, nor never die shall:
Make much of Parrot, the popagay royal.

For that peerless prince that Parrot did create,
He made you of nothing by his majesty.
Point well this problem that Parrot doth prate,
And remember among how Parrot and ye
Shall leap from this life, as merry as we be:

Pomp, pride, honour, riches, and worldly lust,
Parrot saith plainly, shall turn all to dust.

Thus Parrot doth pray you,
    With heart most tender,
230   To reckon with this recueil now,
    And it to remember.

Psittacus, ecce, cano, nec sunt mea carmina Phoebo
Digna scio, tamen est plena camena deo.

Secundum Skeltonida famigeratum,
In Piereorum catalogo numeratum.

Itaque consolamini invicem in verbis istis, &c.
Candidi lectores, callide callete vestrum fovete Psittacum, &c.

Galathea
Speak, Parrot, I pray you, for Mary's sake,
What moan he made when Pamphilus lost his make.

Parrot
240   My proper Bess,
    My pretty Bess,
        Turn once again to me;
    For sleepest thou, Bess,
    Or wakest thou, Bess,
        Mine heart it is with thee.

    My daisy delectable,
    My primrose commendable,
    My violet amiable,
    My joy inexplicable,
250   Now turn again to me.

    I will be firm and stable,
    And to you serviceable,

98

And also profitable,
If ye be agreeable,
   My proper Bess,
    To turn again to me.

Alas, I am disdained,
And as a man half maimed,
My heart is so sore pained,
I pray thee, Bess, unfeigned
    Yet come again to me.

By love I am constrained
To be with you retained,
It will not be refrained:
I pray you, be reclaimed,
   My proper Bess,
    And turn again to me.
Quoth Parrot, thy popagay royal.

Martialis cecinit carmen, fit mihi scutum:
Est mihi lasciva pagina, vita proba.

  Galathea
Now kus me, Parrot, kus me, kus, kus;
God's blessing light on thy little sweet mus!

    Vita et Anima,
    Zoe kai psyche.
Concumbunt Graece. Non est hic sermo pudicus.

Ergo *Attica dictamina*
    Sunt plumbina lamina,
    Vel spuria vitulamina:
    Avertat haec Urania.   *Amen.*

    Amen, Amen,
      And set too a D,

260

270

280

And then it is Amend,
Our new-found A.B.C.

Lenvoy primere
Go, little quire, named the Popagay,
Home to resort Jereboseth persuade;
For the cliffs of Scalop they roar wellaway,
And the sands of Cefas begin to waste and fade,
For replication restless that he of late there made.
290 Now Neptune and Aeolus are agreed of likelihood,
For Titus at Dover abideth in the road;

Lucina she wadeth among the watery floods,
And the cocks begin to crow again the day;
Le toison de Jason is lodged among the shrouds,
Of Argus revenged, recover when he may;
Lyacon of Libyk and Lydy hath caught his prey:
Go, little quire, pray them that you behold,
In their remembrance ye may be enrolled.

Yet some fools say that ye are furnished with knacks,
300 That hang together as feathers in the wind;
But lewdly are they lettered that your learning lacks,
Barking and whining like churlish curs of kind:
For who looketh wisely in your works may find
Much fruitful matter. But now, for your defence,
Again all remords arm you with patience.

Monosticon
Ipse sagax aequi ceu verax nuntius ito.
Morda puros mal desires.
Penultima die Octobris, 33°

Secunde lenvoy
Pass forth, Parrot, towards some passenger;
310 Require him to convey you over the salt foam;
Addressing yourself, like a sad messenger,

To our sullen seignor Sadok, desire him to come home,
Making his pilgrimage by *Nostre Dame de Crome*:
For Jericho and Jersey shall meet together as soon
As he to exploit the man out of the moon.

With purpose and grandpose he may feed him fat,
Though he pamper not his paunch with the Great Seal;
We have longed and looked long time for that,
Which causeth poor suitors have many a hungry meal:
320   As president and regent he ruleth every deal.
Now pass forth, good Parrot, our Lord be your steed,
In this your journey to prosper and speed.

And though some disdain you, and say how ye prate,
And how your poems are barren of polished eloquence,
There is none that your name will abrogate
Than nodipolls and gramatolls of small intelligence;
Too rude is their reason to reach to your sentence.
Such melancholy mastiffs and mangy cur dogs
Are meet for a swineherd to hunt after hogs.

Monosticon
330   *Psittace, perge volans, fatuorum tela retundas.*
Morda puros mal desires.
In diebus Novembris
34.

Le dereyn lenvoy
Prepare you, Parrot, bravely your passage to take,
Of Mercury under the trinal aspect,
And sadly salute our sullen Sydrake,
And show him that all the world doth conject
How the matters he mells in come to small effect;
For he wanteth of his wits that all would rule alone;
It is no little burden to bear a great mill-stone.

340   To bring all the sea into a cherrystone pit,
To number all the stars in the firmament,

To rule nine realms by one man's wit,
To such things impossible reason cannot consent.
Much money, men say, there madly he hath spent:
Parrot, ye may prate this under protestation,
Was never such a senator since Christ's incarnation.

Wherefore he may now come again as he went,
Non sine postica sanna, as I trow,
From Calais to Dover, to Canterbury in Kent,
350   To make reckoning in the receipt how Robin lost his bow,
To sow corn in the sea-sand, there will no crop grow.
Though ye be taunted, Parrot, with tongues attainted,
Yet your problems are pregnant, and with loyalty acquainted.

       Monosticon
   I, properans Parrote, malas sic corripe linguas.
     Morda puros mal desires.
      15 Kalendis Decembris,
      34.

       Dysticon miserabile
   Altior, heu, cedroe, crudelior, heu, leopardo;
   Heu, vitulus bubali fit dominus Priami!

       Tetrasticon
   Non annis licet et Priamus sed honore voceris:
360   *Dum foveas vitulum, rex, regeris, Britonum;*
   Rex, regeris, non ipse regis: rex inclyte, calle;
   Subde tibi vitulum ne fatuet nimium.

      God amend all,
         That all amend may!
      Amen, quoth Parrot,
         The royal popagay.

   Kalendis Decembris
   34.

Lenvoy royalle

Go, proper Parrot, my popagay,
That lords and ladies this pamphlet may behold,
370 With notable clerks: supply to them, I pray,
Your rudeness to pardon, and also that they would
Vouchsafe to defend you again the brawling scold
Called Detraction, encankered with envy,
Whose tongue is attainted with slanderous obloquy.

For truth in parable ye wantonly pronounce,
Language divers, yet under that doth rest
Matter more precious than the rich jacounce,
Diamond, or ruby, or balas of the best,
Or Indy sapphire with orient pearls dressed.
380 Wherefore your remorders are mad, or else stark blind,
You to remord erst ere they know your mind.

Disticon
I, volitans, Parrote, tuam moderare Minervam:
   Vix tua percipient, qui tua teque legent.

Hyperbaton
Psittacus hi notus seu Persius est, puto, notus,
Nec, reor, est nec erit, licet est erit.
   Maledite soit bouche malheureuse!
      34.

Laucture de Parott
O my Parrot, *O unice dilecte, votorum meorum omnis lapis,*
   lapis pretiosus operimentum tuum!

Parrot
   Sicut Aaron populumque,
     Sic bubali vitulus,
390   *Sic bubali vitulus,*
     Sic bubali vitulus.
Thus much Parrot hath openly expressed—
Let see who dare make up the rest.

Le Popagay s'en va complaindre
Helas! I lament the dull abused brain,
The infatuate fantasies, the witless wilfulness
Of one and other at me that have disdain.
Some say they cannot my parables express;
Some say I rail at riot reckless;
Some say but little and think more in their thought,
400 How this process I prate of it is not all for nought.

O causeless cowards, O heartless hardiness,
O manless manhood, enfainted all with fear,
O cunning clergy, where is your readiness
To practise or postil this process here and there?
For dread ye dare not meddle with such gear,
Or else ye pinch courtesy, truly as I trow,
Which of you first dare boldly pluck the crow.

The sky is cloudy, the coast is nothing clear;
Titan hath trussed up his tresses of fine gold;
410 Jupiter for Saturn dare make no royal cheer;
Lyacon laugheth thereat, and beareth him more bold;
Rachel, ruely ragged, she is like to catch cold;
Moloch, that mawmet, there dare no man withstay—
The rest of such reckoning may make a foul fray.

　　　Dixit, quoth Parrot, the royal popagay.

Parrot
Jupiter ut nitido deus est veneratus Olympo;
　　Hic coliturque deus.
Sunt data thura Jovi, rutilo solio residenti;
　　Cum Jove thura capit.
420 *Jupiter astrorum rector dominusque polorum,*
　　Anglica sceptra regit.

　　Galathea
I compass the conveyance unto the capital
Of our clerk Cleros, whither, thither, and why not hither?

For pass-a-Pace apace is gone to catch a moll,
Over Scarpary *mala vi*, Monsieur cy-and-slidder:
What sequel shall follow when pendugums meet together?
Speak, Parrot, my sweet bird, and ye shall have a date,
Of franticness and foolishness which is the great state?

Parrot

Difficile it is to answer this demand;
430 Yet, after the sagacity of a popagay,
Franticness doth rule and all thing command;
Wilfulness and brainless now rule all the ray;
Again frantic frenzy there dare no man say nay,
For franticness and wilfulness, and brainless ensemble,
The nebbis of a lion they make to treat and tremble,

To jumble, to stumble, to tumble down like fools,
To lour, to droop, to kneel, to stoop, and to play couch quail,
To fish afore the net and to draw pools;
He maketh them to bear baubles, and to bear a low sail;
440 He carrieth a king in his sleeve, if all the world fail;
He faceth out at a flush with, 'show, take all!'
Of Pope Julius' cards he is chief cardinal.

He triumpheth, he trumpeth, he turneth all up and down,
With, 'skirgalliard, proud palliard, vauntparler, ye prate!'
His wolf's head, wan, blue as lead, gapeth over the crown—
It is to fear lest he would wear the garland on his pate,
Paregal with all princes far passing his estate;
For of our regent the regiment he hath, *ex qua vi*,
Patet per versus quod ex vi bolte harvi.

450 Now, Galathea, let Parrot, I pray you, have his date—
Yet dates now are dainty, and wax very scant,
For grocers were grudged at and groaned at but late;
Great raisins with reasons be now reprobitant,
For raisins are no reasons, but reasons currant.

Run God, run Devil! Yet the date of our Lord
And the date of the Devil doth surely accord.

Dixit, quoth Parrot, the popagay royal.

Galathea
Now, Parrot, my sweet bird, speak out yet once again,
Set aside all sophisms, and speak now true and plain.

Parrot
460 So many moral matters, and so little used;
So much new making, and so mad time spent;
So much translation into English confused;
So much noble preaching, and so little amendment;
So much consultation, almost to none intent;
So much provision, and so little wit at need—
Since Deucalion's flood there can no clerks read.

So little discretion, and so much reasoning;
So much hardy-dardy, and so little manliness;
So prodigal expense, and so shameful reckoning;
470 So gorgeous garments, and so much wretchedness;
So much portly pride, with purses penniless;
So much spent before, and so much unpaid behind—
Since Deucalion's flood there can no clerks find.

So much forecasting, and so far an after deal;
So much politic prating, and so little standeth in stead;
So little secretness, and so much great counsel;
So many bold barons, their hearts as dull as lead;
So many noble bodies under one daw's head;
So royal a king as reigneth upon us all—
480 Since Deucalion's flood was never seen nor shall.

So many complaints, and so small redress;
So much calling on, and so small taking heed;
So much loss of merchandise, and so remediless;
So little care for the common weal, and so much need;

So much doubtful danger, and so little dread;
So much pride of prelates, so cruel and so keen—
Since Deucalion's flood, I trow, was never seen.

So many thieves hanged, and thieves nevertheless;
So much prisonment for matters not worth an haw;
490   So much papers wearing for right a small excess;
So much pillory pageants under colour of good law;
So much turning on the cuck-stool for every gee-gaw;
So much mockish making of Statutes of Array—
Since Deucalion's flood was never, I dare say.

So brainless calves' heads, so many sheep's tails;
So bold a bragging butcher, and flesh sold so dear;
So many plucked partridges, and so fat quails;
So mangy a mastiff cur, the great greyhound's peer;
So big a bulk of brow-antlers cabbaged that year;
500   So many swans dead, and so small revel—
Since Deucalion's flood, I trow, no man can tell.

So many truces taken, and so little perfect truth;
So much belly-joy, and so wasteful banqueting;
So pinching and sparing, and so little profit groweth;
So many huge houses building, and so small householding;
Such statutes upon diets, such pilling and polling;
So is all thing wrought wilfully without reason and skill—
Since Deucalion's flood the world was never so ill.

So many vagabonds, so many beggars bold;
510   So much decay of monasteries and of religious places;
So hot hatred against the Church, and charity so cold;
So much of 'my Lord's grace,' and in him no grace is;
So many hollow hearts, and so double faces;
So much sanctuary breaking, and privileged barred—
Since Deucalion's flood was never seen nor lyerd.

So much ragged right of a ram's horn;
So rigorous revelling in a prelate specially;

So bold and so bragging, and was so basely born;
So lordly in his looks, and so disdainously;
520 So fat a maggot, bred of a flesh-fly;
Was never such a filthy gorgon, nor such an epicure,
Since Deucalion's flood, I make thee fast and sure.

So much privy watching in cold winters' nights;
So much searching of losels, and is himself so lewd;
So much conjurations for elfish mid-day sprites;
So many bulls of pardon published and showed;
So much crossing and blessing, and him all beshrewed;
Such pole-axes and pillars, such mules trapt with gold—
Since Deucalion's flood in no chronicle is told.

>*Dixit*, quoth Parrot.

530 *Crescet in immensum me vivo Psitaccus iste;*
Hinc mea dicetur Skeltonidis inclita fama.
Quoth Skelton Laureat,
Orator Regius
34.

from THE GARLAND OF LAUREL

1-448 Musing on mortality, Skelton goes to sleep against the stump of a tree. He dreams of a pavilion occupied by the Queen of Fame, the earthly representative of Dame Pallas. The Queen and the goddess debate Skelton's worthiness to be included in Fame's court.

Dame Pallas commanded that they should me convey
450 Into the rich palace of the Queen of Fame:
'There shall he hear what she will to him say
When he is called to answer to his name.'
A cry anon forthwith she made proclaim,
All orators and poets should thither go before,
With all the press that there was less and more.

Forthwith, I say, thus wandering in my thought,
How it was, or else within what hours,
I cannot tell you, but that I was brought
Into a palace with turrets and towers,
460 Engalleried goodly with halls and bowers,
So curiously, so craftily, so cunningly wrought
That all this world, I trow, and it were sought,

Such another there could no man find;
Whereof partly I purpose to expound,
Whiles it remaineth fresh in my mind.
With turquoise and chrysolites enpaved was the ground;
Of beryl embossed were the pillars round;
Of elephants' teeth were the palace gates,
Enlozenged with many goodly plates

470 Of gold, entached with many a precious stone;
An hundred steps mounting to the hall,
One of jasper, another of whalesbone;
Of diamonds pointed was the rocky wall;
The carpets within and tapettes of pall;
The chambers hanged with clothes of Arras;
Envaulted with rubies the vault was of this place.

Thus passed we forth walking unto the pretory
Where the posts were enbullioned with sapphires Indy blue,
Englazed glittering with many a clear story;
480 Jacinths and smaragds out of the florth they grew.
Unto this place all poets there did sue,
Wherein was set of Fame the noble Queen,
All other transcending, most richly beseen,

Under a glorious cloth of estate,
Fret all with orient pearls of garnate,
Encrowned as empress of all this worldly fate,
So royally, so richly, so passingly ornate,
It was exceeding beyond the common rate.

This house environ was a mile about;
490   If twelve were let in, twelve hundred stood without.

Then to this lady and sovereign of this palace
Of pursuivants there pressed in with many a diverse tale;
Some were of Poyle, and some were of Thrace,
Of Limerick, of Lorraine, of Spain, of Portingale,
From Naples, from Navern, and from Rouncevale,
Some from Flanders, some from the sea coast,
Some from the mainland, some from the French host:

With, 'how doth the north?' 'What tidings in the south?'
'The west is windy;' 'the east is meetly wele,'
500   It is hard to tell of every man's mouth;
A slippery hold the tail is of an eel,
And he halteth often that hath a kiby heel.
Some showed his safe-conduct, some showed his charter,
Some looked full smoothly, and had a false quarter;

With, 'sir, I pray you, a little time stand back,
And let me come in to deliver my letter.'
Another told how ships went to wrack;
There were many words smaller and greater,
With, 'I as good as thou!' 'I'faith and no better!'
510   Some came to tell truth, some came to lie,
Some came to flatter, and some came to spy.

There were, I say, of all manner of sorts,
Of Dartmouth, of Plymouth, of Portsmouth also;
The burgess and the bailiffs of the five ports,
With, 'now let me come,' and, 'now let me go,'
And all time wandered I thus to and fro,
Till at the last these noble poets three
Unto me said, 'lo, sir, now ye may see

'Of this high court the daily business.
520   From you must we, but not long to tarry.

Lo, hither cometh a goodly mistress,
Occupation, Fame's registrary,
Which shall be to you a sovereign accessory,
With singular pleasures to drive away the time,
And we shall see you again ere it be prime.'

526-601 Occupation welcomes Skelton and takes him to a wall which has a thousand gates built into it.

Then I me leant, and looked over the wall.
Innumerable people pressed to every gate.
Shut were the gates; they might well knock and call,
And turn home again, for they came all too late.
I her demanded of them and their estate.
'Forsooth,' quoth she, 'they be haskards and ribalds,
Dicers, carders, tumblers with gambolds,

'Furtherers of love, with bawdry acquainted,
610   Brainless blinkards that blow at the coal,
False forgers of money, for coinage attainted,
Pope-holy hypocrites, as they were gold and whole,
Pole-hatchets, that prate will at every ale-pole,
Riot, reveller, railer, bribery, theft,
With other conditions that well might be left.

'Some feign themselves fools, and would be called wise,
Some meddling spies, by craft to grope thy mind,
Some disdainous dawcocks that all men despise,
False flatterers that fawn thee, and curs of kind
620   That speak fair before thee and shrewdly behind;
Hither they come crowding to get them a name,
But haled they be homeward with sorrow and shame.'

With that I heard guns rush out at once:
'Bounce, bounce, bounce!' that all they out cried;
It made some limp-legged and bruised their bones;
Some were made peevish, porishly pink-eyed,

That ever more after by it they were espied;
And one there was there, I wondered of his hap,
For a gun-stone, I say, had all to-jagged his cap:

630 Ragged and dagged, and cunningly cut,
The blast of the brimstone blew away his brain;
Mazed as a March hare, he ran like a scut;
And, sir, among all methought I saw twain:
The one was a tumbler, that afterward again
Of a dicer, a devil way, grew a gentleman,
Pierce Prater the second, that quarrels began.

With a pellet of peevishness they had such a stroke,
That all the days of their life shall stick by their ribs!
Foo, foisty bawdias! some smelled of the smoke!
640 I saw divers that were carried away thence in cribs,
Dazing after dotterels, like drunkards that dribs.
These titivels with tampions were touched and tapped;
Much mischief, I hight you, among them there happed.

Sometime, as it seemeth, when the moon-light
By means of a grossly endarked cloud
Suddenly is eclipsed in the winter night,
In like manner of wise a mist did us shroud.
But well may ye think I was nothing proud
Of that adventure, which made me sore aghast.
650 In darkness thus dwelt we, till at the last

The clouds 'gan to clear, the mist was rarified;
In an herber I saw, brought where I was,
There birds on the briar sang on every side;
With alleys ensanded about in compass,
The banks enturfed with singular solace,
Enrailed with rosers, and vines engraped;
It was a new comfort of sorrows escaped.

658-772 In the garden Skelton sees a goodly laurel tree growing, from which garlands are made by dryads and the nine muses. Occupation takes him to see the Countess of Surrey, surrounded by a bevy of ladies.

'Come forth, gentlewomen, I pray you,' she said,
'I have contrived for you a goodly work,
And who can work best now shall be assayed.
A coronal of laurel with verdures light and dark
I have devised for Skelton, my clerk;
For to his service I have such regard,
That of our bounty we will him reward.

780 'For of all ladies he hath the library,
Their names recounting in the court of Fame;
Of all gentlewomen he hath the scrutiny,
In Fame's court reporting the same;
For yet of women he never said shame,
But if they were counterfeits, that women them call,
That list of their lewdness with him for to brawl.'

With that the tapettes and carpets were laid
Whereon these ladies softly might rest,
The sampler to sow on, the laces to enbraid;
790 To weave in the stole some were full prest,
With sleys, with tavelles, with hiddles well dressed;
The frame was brought forth with his weaving pin—
God give them good speed their work to begin!

Some to embroider put them in press,
Well guiding their glowton to keep straight their silk,
Some pirling of gold their work to increase
With fingers small, and hands white as milk;
With, 'reach me that skein of tully silk,'
And, 'wind me that bottom of such an hue'—
800 Green, red, tawny, white, black, purple, and blue.

113

Of broken works wrought many a goodly thing,
In casting, in turning, in flourishing of flowers,
With burrs rough and bottons surfeling,
In needle-work raising birds in bowers,
With virtue enbusied all times and hours;
And truly of their bounty thus were they bent
To work me this chaplet of good advisement.

Occupation to Skelton
Behold and see in your advertisement
How these ladies and gentlewomen all
810   For your pleasure do their endeavourment,
And for your sake how fast to work they fall:
To your remembrance wherefore ye must call
In goodly words pleasantly comprised,
That for them some goodly conceit be devised,

With proper captations of benevolence,
Ornately polished after your faculty,
Sith ye must needs aforce it by pretence
Of your profession unto humanity,
Commencing your process after their degree,
820   To each of them rendering thanks commendable,
With sentence fructuous and terms convenable.

Poeta Skelton
Advancing myself some thank to deserve,
I me determined for to sharp my pen,
Devoutly arecting my prayer to Minerva,
She to vouchsafe me to inform and ken;
To Mercury also heartily prayed I then,
Me to support, to help, and to assist,
To guide and to govern my dreadful trembling fist.

As a mariner that amazed is in a stormy rage,
830   Hardly bestead and driven is to hope
Of that the tempestuous wind will assuage,

114

In trust whereof comfort his heart doth grope,
From the anchor he cutteth the cable-rope,
Commiteth all to God, and letteth his ship ride,
So I beseech Jesu now to be my guide!

To the right noble Countess of Surrey
After all duly ordered obeisance,
In humble wise, as lowly as I may,
Unto you, madam, I make reconusance.
My life enduring, I shall both write and say,
840 Recount, report, rehearse without delay
The passing bounty of your noble estate,
Of honour and worship which hath the former date.

Like to Argyva by just resemblance,
The noble wife of Polymites king;
Prudent Rebecca, of whom remembrance
The Bible maketh; with whose chaste living
Your noble demeanour is counterweighing,
Whose passing bounty, and right noble estate,
Of honour and worship it hath the former date.

850 The noble Pamphila, queen of the Greeks' land,
Habiliments royal found out industriously;
Thamer also wrought with her goodly hand
Many devices passing curiously;
Whom ye represent and exemplify,
Whose passing bounty, and right noble estate,
Of honour and worship it hath the former date.

As Dame Thamarys, which took the king of Perce,
Cyrus by name, as writeth the story;
Dame Agrippina also I may rehearse,
860 Of gentle courage the perfect memory;
So shall your name endure perpetually,
Whose passing bounty, and right noble estate,
Of honour and worship it hath the former date.

To my lady Elisabeth Howard
To be your remembrancer, madam, I am bound,
Like to Aryna, maidenly of port,
Of virtue and cunning the well and perfect ground;
Whom Dame Nature, as well I may report,
Hath freshly enbeautied with many a goodly sort
Of womanly features, whose flourishing tender age
870   Is lusty to look on, pleasant, demure, and sage.

Goodly Crisseid, fairer than Polyxene,
For to envive Pandarus' appetite;
Troilus, I trow, if that he had you seen,
In you he would have set his whole delight.
Of all your beauty I suffice not to write;
But, as I said, your flourishing tender age
Is lusty to look on, pleasant, demure, and sage.

To my lady Muriel Howard
My little lady I may not leave behind,
But do her service needs now I must;
880   Benign, courteous, of gentle heart and mind,
Whom Fortune and Fate plainly have discussed
Long to enjoy pleasure, delight, and lust:
The enbudded blossoms of roses red of hue,
With lilies white your beauty doth renew.

Compare you I may to Cydippes, the maid,
That of Acontius, when she found the bill
In her bosom, lord, how she was afraid!
The ruddy shamefacedness in her visage fill,
Which manner of abashment became her not ill.
890   Right so, madam, the roses red of hue
With lilies white your beauty doth renew.

To my lady Anne Dacres of the South
Zeuxis that enpictured fair Helen the queen,
You to devise his craft were to seek;

116

And if Apelles your countenance had seen,
Of portraiture which was the famous Greek,
He could not devise the least point of your cheek.
Princess of youth, and flower of goodly port,
Virtue, cunning, solace, pleasure, comfort.

Paregal in honour unto Penelope,
900   That for her truth is in remembrance had;
Fair Deianira surmounting in beauty;
Demure Diana womanly and sad,
Whose lusty looks make heavy hearts glad.
Princess of youth, and flower of goodly port,
Virtue, cunning, solace, pleasure, comfort.

To mistress Margery Wentworth
   With marjoram gentle,
The flower of goodlihead,
Embroidered the mantle
Is of your maidenhead.
910   Plainly I cannot glose;
Ye be, as I divine,
The pretty primrose,
The goodly columbine.
   With marjoram gentle,
The flower of goodlihead,
Embroidered the mantle
Is of your maidenhead.
   Benign, courteous, and meek,
With words well devised;
920   In you, who list to seek,
Be virtues well comprised.
   With marjoram gentle,
The flower of goodlihead,
Embroidered the mantle
Is of your maidenhead.

To mistress Margaret Tilney

I you assure,
Full well I know
My busy cure
To you I owe;
930   Humbly and low
Commending me
To your bounty.
    As Machareus
Fair Canace,
So I, ywis,
Endeavour me
Your name to see
It be enrolled,
Written with gold.
940   Phaedra ye may
Well represent;
Intentive aye
And diligent,
No time misspent;
Wherefore delight
I have to write
    Of Margarite
Pearl orient,
Lodestar of light,
950   Much relucent;
Madam regent
I may you call
Of virtues all.

To mistress Jane Blennerhasset

What though my pen wax faint,
And hath small lust to paint:
Yet shall there no restraint
Cause me to cease,
Among this press,
For to increase

118

960   Your goodly name.
       I will myself apply,
Trust me, intentively,
You for to stellify;
And so observe
That ye ne swerve
For to deserve
Immortal fame.
    Sith mistress Jane Hasset
Small flowers helped to set
970   In my goodly chaplet,
Therefore I render of her the memory
Unto the legend of fair Laodamy.

To mistress Isabel Pennell
    By Saint Mary, my lady,
Your mammy and your daddy
Brought forth a goodly baby!
    My maiden Isabel,
Reflaring rosabel,
The fragrant camomel,
    The ruddy rosary,
980   The sovereign rosemary,
The pretty strawberry,
    The columbine, the nept,
The jelofer well set,
The proper violet:
    Ennewed your colour
Is like the daisy flower
After the April shower;
    Star of the morrow grey,
The blossom on the spray,
990   The freshest flower of May;
    Maidenly demure,
Of womanhood the lure;
Wherefore I make you sure
    It were an heavenly health,

It were an endless wealth,
A life for God himself,
　　To hear this nightingale
Among the birds small
Warbling in the vale,
Dug, dug,
Jug, jug,
Good year and good luck,
With chuck, chuck, chuck, chuck.

To mistress Margaret Hussey
　　Merry Margaret,
As midsummer flower,
Gentle as falcon
Or hawk of the tower:
　　With solace and gladness,
Much mirth and no madness,
All good and no badness;
So joyously,
So maidenly,
So womanly,
Her demeaning
In every thing,
Far, far passing,
That I can indite,
Or suffice to write
Of merry Margaret
As midsummer flower,
Gentle as falcon
Or hawk of the tower:
　　As patient and still
And as full of good will
As fair Isaphill,
Coriander,
Sweet pomander,
Good Cassander,
Steadfast of thought,

1000

1010

1020

1030   Well made, well wrought,
        Far may be sought
        Erst that ye can find
        So courteous, so kind
        As merry Margaret,
        This midsummer flower,
        Gentle as falcon
        Or hawk of the tower.

To mistress Gertrude Statham
        Though ye were hard-hearted,
        And I with you thwarted
1040   With words that smarted,
        Yet now doubtless ye give me cause
        To write of you this goodly clause,
        Mistress Gertrude,
        With womanhood endued,
        With virtue well renewed.
        I will that ye shall be
        In all benignity
        Like to Dame Pasiphae;
        For now doubtless ye give me cause
1050   To write of you this goodly clause,
        Mistress Gertrude,
        With womanhood endued,
        With virtue well renewed.
        Partly by your counsel,
        Garnished with laurel
        Was my fresh coronal;
        Wherefore doubtless ye give me cause
        To write of you this goodly clause,
        Mistress Gertrude,
1060   With womanhood endued,
        With virtue well renewed.

But if I should aquite your kindness,
   Else say ye might
That in me were great blindness
I for to be so mindless
And could not write
Of Isabel Knight.
   It is not my custom nor my guise
To leave behind
1070   Her that is both womanly and wise,
And specially which glad was to devise
The means to find
To please my mind
   In helping to work my laurel green
With silk and gold:
Galathea, the maid well beseen,
   Was never half so fair, as I ween,
Which was extolled
A thousandfold
1080   By Maro, the Mantuan prudent,
Who list to read.
But, and I had leisure competent
I could show you such a precedent
In very deed
How ye exceed.

1086-1148 Skelton comes before the Queen of Fame. She frowns at the garland he wears and asks what he has done to deserve it. Occupation offers to present Skelton's case for wearing the laurel.

The Queen of Fame to Occupation
Your book of remembrance we will now that ye read,
1150   If any records in number can be found,
What Skelton hath compiled and written in deed,
Rehearsing by order, and what is the ground,
Let see now for him how ye can expound;

For in our court, ye wot well, his name cannot rise
But if he write oftener than once or twice.

Skelton Poeta
With that, of the book loosened were the clasps:
The margin was illumined all with golden rails
And byse, enpictured with gressops and wasps,
With butterflies, and fresh peacock tails,
1160   Enflored with flowers and slimy snails;
Envived pictures well touched and quickly;
It would have made a man whole that had been right sickly

To behold how it was garnished and bound,
Encovered over with gold of tissue fine;
The clasps and bullions were worth a thousand pound;
With balasses and carbuncles the borders did shine;
With *aurum mosaicum* every other line
Was written. And so she did her speed,
Occupation, immediately to read.

*Occupation readeth and expoundeth some part of Skelton's books
and ballads with ditties of pleasure . . .*

1170   Of your orator and poet laureate
Of England, his works here they begin:
In primis, the Book of Honourous Estate;
Item, the book how men should flee sin;
Item, Royal Demeanance worship to win;
Item, the book to speak well or be still;
Item, to learn you to die when ye will;

Of virtue also the sovereign interlude;
The Book of the Rosiar; Prince Arthur's Creation;
The False Faith that now goeth, which daily is renewed;
1180   Item, his Dialogues of Imagination;
Item, Automedon of Love's Meditation;
Item, New Grammar in English compiled;
Item, Bouge of Court, where Drede was beguiled;

His comedy, Achademios called by name;
Of Tully's Familiars the translation;
Item, Good Advisement, that brainless doth blame;
The Recule against Gaguin of the French nation;
Item, the Popingay, that hath in commendation
Ladies and gentlewomen such as deserved,
1190   And such as be counterfeits they be reserved;

And of Sovereignty a noble pamphlet;
And of Magnificence a notable matter,
How Counterfeit Countenance of the new jet
With Crafty Conveyance doth smatter and flatter,
And Cloaked Collusion is brought in to clatter
With Courtly Abusion; who printeth it well in mind
Much doubleness of the world therein he may find;

Of Mannerly Mistress Margery Milk and Ale,
To her he wrote many matters of mirth;
1200   Yet, though I say it, thereby lieth a tale,
For Margery winched, and brake her hinder girth:
Lor, how she made much of her gentle birth!
With, 'gingerly, go gingerly!' her tail was made of hay;
Go she never so gingerly, her honesty is gone away!

Hard to make ought of that is naked nought;
This fustian mistress and this giggish gase,
Wonder is to write what wrenches she wrought,
To face out her folly with a midsummer maze;
With pitch she patched her pitcher should not craze—
1210   It may well rhyme, but shrewdly it doth accord,
To pick out honesty of such a potsherd!
*   *   *   *   *   *

Of my lady's grace at the contemplation,
1220   Out of French into English prose,
Of Man's Life the Peregrination
He did translate, interpret, and disclose;
The Treatise of Triumphs of the Red Rose,

Wherein many stories are briefly contained,
That unremembered long time remained.

The Duke of York's creancer when Skelton was,
Now Henry the Eighth, King of England,
A treatise he devised and brought it to pass,
Called *Speculum Principis*, to bear in his hand,
1230   Therein to read and to understand
All the demeanour of princely estate,
To be our king, of God preordinate;

Also the Tunning of Elinour Rumming,
With Colin Clout, John Ive, with Joforth Jack—
To make such trifles it asketh some cunning,
In honest mirth pardee requireth no lack;
The white appeareth the better for the black,
After conveyance as the world goes,
It is no folly to use the Welshman's hose;

1240   The umbles of venison, the bottle of wine,
To fair mistress Anne that should have been sent,
He wrote thereof many a pretty line,
Where it became, and whither it went,
And how that it was wantonly spent;
The Ballad also of the Mustard Tart—
Such problems to paint, it longeth to his art;

Of one Adam all a knave, late dead and gone—
Dormiat in pace, like a dormouse—
He wrote an Epitaph for his grave-stone,
1250   With words devout and sentence agerdouce,
For he was ever against God's house:
All his delight was to brawl and to bark
Against Holy Church, the priest, and the clerk.

Of Philip Sparrow, the lamentable fate,
The doleful destiny, and the careful chance,

Devised by Skelton after the funeral rate;
Yet some there be therewith that take grievance,
And grudge thereat with frowning countenance;
But what of that! hard it is to please all men—
1260   Who list amend it, let him set to his pen.

     *   *   *   *   *   *

1310   Though Galen and Dioscorides,
With Hippocras and master Avicen,
By their physic doth many a man ease,
And though Albumasar can thee inform and ken
What constellations are good or bad for men,
Yet when the rain raineth and the goose winketh,
Little wotteth the gosling what the goose thinketh.

He is not wise again the stream that striveth;
Dun is in the mire, dame, reach me my spur;
Needs must he run that the devil driveth;
1320   When the steed is stolen, spar the stable door;
A gentle hound should never play the cur;
It is soon espied where the thorn pricketh,
And well wotteth the cat whose beard she licketh;

With Marion clarion, sol, lucern,
Grand juir, of this French proverb old,
How men were wont for to discern
By Candlemas Day what weather should hold,
But Marion clarion was caught with a cold,
1330   And all overcast with clouds unkind,
This goodly flower with storms was untwined;

This jelofer gentle, this rose, this lily flower,
This primrose peerless, this proper violet,
This columbine clear and freshest of colour,
This delicate daisy, this strawberry prettily set,
With froward frosts, alas, was all to-fret!
But who may have a more ungracious life
Than a child's bird and a knave's wife?

Think what ye will
1340 Of this wanton bill;
By Mary Gipsy,
Quod scripsi, scripsi:
Uxor tua, sicut vitis,
Habetis in custodiam,
Custodite sicut scitis,
Secundum Lucam, etc.

Of the Bonhams of Ashridge beside Berkhamstead,
That goodly place to Skelton most kind,
Where the sang royal is, Christ's blood so red,
Whereupon he metrified after his mind—
1350 A pleasanter place than Ashridge is hard were to find,
As Skelton rehearseth, with words few and plain,
In his distichon made on verses twain:

Fraxinus in clivo frondetque viret sine rivo,
Non est sub divo similis sine flumine vivo.

The Nation of Fools he left not behind;
Item, Apollo that whirled up his chair,
That made some to snur and snuff in the wind;
It made them to skip, to stamp, and to stare,
Which, if they be happy, have cause to beware
1360 In rhyming and railing with him for to mell,
For dread that he learn them their A, B, C, to spell.

Poeta Skelton
With that I stood up, half suddenly afraid;
Supplying to Fame, I besought her grace,
And that it would please her, full tenderly I prayed
Out of her books Apollo to rase.
'Nay sir,' she said, 'whatso in this place
Of our noble court is once spoken out,
It must needs after run all the world about.'

God wot, these words made me full sad;
1370   And when that I saw it would no better be,
But that my petition would not be had,
What should I do but take it in gre?
For, by Jupiter and his high majesty,
I did what I could to scrape out the scrolls,
Apollo to rase out of her ragman rolls.

Now hereof it irketh me longer to write;
To Occupation I will again resort,
Which read on still, as it came to her sight,
Rendering my devices I made in disport
1380   Of the Maiden of Kent called Comfort,
Of lovers' testaments and of their wanton wills,
And how Jolas loved goodly Phylis;

Diodorus Siculus of my translation,
Out of fresh Latin into our English plain,
Recounting commodities of many a strange nation;
Who readeth it once would read it again;
Six volumes engrossed together it doth contain.
But when of the laurel she made rehearsal,
All orators and poets, with other great and small,

1390   A thousand thousand, I trow, to my doom,
'Triumpha, triumpha!' they cried all about;
Of trumpets and clarions the noise went to Rome;
The starry heaven methought shook with the shout,
The ground groaned and trembled, the noise was so stout.
The Queen of Fame commanded shut fast the book,
And therewith suddenly out of my dream I woke.

My mind of the great din was somedeal amazed,
I wiped mine eyen for to make them clear;
Then to the heaven spherical upward I gazed,
1400   Where I saw Janus, with his double cheer,
Making his almanac for the new year;

He turned his tirikis, his volvel ran fast:
Good luck this new year, the old year is past.

*   *   *   *   *   *

Out of Latin into English
    Justice now is dead;
    Truth with a drowsy head,
    As heavy as the lead,
    Is laid down to sleep,
    And taketh no keep:
    And Right is over the fallows
    Gone to seek hallows,
    With Reason together,
    No man can tell whither.
    No man will undertake
    The first twain to wake;
    And the twain last
    Be withhold so fast
    With money, as men sayn,
    They cannot come again.

'Woefully Arrayed', p. 21

Found only in manuscript versions; like the next four poems its date of composition is uncertain, probably the mid or late 1490s. The primary meaning of *arrayed* is 'treated', but it has a cluster of secondary meanings including 'set out' (i.e. on the cross), 'dressed', and 'prepared'. See l. 50 where the word is turned from Christ to man. The attribution of the poem to Skelton has been questioned.

'My Darling Dear', p. 23

A secular parody of a lullaby carol. Printed in *Dyvers Balettys and Dyties Solacyous*, c. 1526.

'The Ancient Acquaintance', p. 24

Printed in *Dyvers Balettys* . . .

16   Two puns: curtals and nags are horses and, respectively, tunic and testicles.

23   *keyleth with a clench* pun: 'kills with her hoof' and 'cools down after an embrace'.

24   *hueth* pun: 'blush' and 'close her legs'.

'Mannerly Margery' p. 25

Found in ms. *Mannerly* means 'polite', 'well behaved', 'affected'.

'Womanhood, Wanton, Ye Want', p. 26

Printed in *Skelton Laureate agaynste a comely Coystrowne*, c. 1526. The surviving poem of those which Skelton wrote to Mistress Anne; see 'Garland of Laurel' ll.1241-2.

'The Bouge of Court', p. 27

First printed 1499. *Bouge* is a corruption of *bouche*, 'food ration', 'wages'.

301-3 *Johan Dawes* and *Doctor Dawcock* names similar in meaning to Simple Simon.

315   Proverb, to bluff.

355   i.e. he dressed as lightly as if it were summer.

361   *so nigh* so threadbare that it barely covered his skin.

365   i.e. while singing hymns he accompanied himself by beating on a pot.

386-7   i.e. cheer up and let's have a couple of drinks at the ale-house.

477   i.e. I have something in my pouch which will shut them up.

'Philip Sparrow', p. 39
First printed c.1545; probably written c.1505.

1   *Placebo* the beginning of the Vespers of the Office of the Dead. The whole poem is punctuated by phrases from the Office; the Psalm texts are taken from the Vulgate.

3   *Dilexi* Psalm 116:1, 'I took pleasure (because the Lord has heard my voice . . .)'

8   *Carrow* a Benedictine priory, near Norwich and the home of Jane Scrope the speaker in this part of the poem.

64   'Woe, woe is me.'

66   Ps.120:1, 'In my distress I cried unto the Lord . . .'

97   Ps.121:1, 'I lifted my eyes unto the hills . . .'

143-5   Ps.130:3,1, 'If iniquities (thou will mark, O Lord . . .)'; 'Out of the depths I have cried (unto thee, O Lord). . .'

183-5   Ps.138:8,1, 'the works (of your hands, do not forsake)'; 'I will confess to you, O Lord, with all my heart.'

239   'From the gates of hell . . .'

243   'I heard a voice . . .'

247   *Armony* Armenia, where Noah's ark settled.

294   *manticors* fabulous monsters, with the body of a lion, head of a man, porcupine's quills, and tail of a scorpion.

386   Ps.146:1, 'Praise the Lord, O my soul!'

441   *the Grail* the Gradual, which comes between the Epistle (l.425) and the Gospel (l.423).

489-90   'Lest by singing badly . . .'

532   'Deliver me . . .'

534   *bemole* sing B flat

575   'Give them eternal rest, O Lord.'

579   Ps.26:13, 'I believe I shall see the goodness of the Lord.'

581   'Lord, listen to my prayer.'

586   'God, whose nature it is to show mercy and to spare.'

826-33 'Sweet flower of birds, farewell! Philip, you rest now beneath this marble, you who were my dear one. Like the shining stars in the dark heavens you will always be set in my heart.'

834-43 'By me, Skelton, the laureate poet of Britain, it is proper to sing these things, under a fictional likeness of her whose bird you were, the maiden of excellent body. Nais was fair, Joan is more beautiful; Corinna was clever, but she is wise.'

845 Ps.119:1, 'Blessed are the undefiled in the way (who walk in the law of the Lord).'

898 'This twin of purity.'

900 Ps.119:17, 'Deal bountifully with thy servant, that I may live . . .'

901 Ps.63:3, '(Because thy lovingkindness is better than life,) my lips shall praise thee.'

996 Ps.119:33, 'Teach me, O Lord, the way of thy statutes . . .'

997 Ps.42:1, 'As the hart panteth after the water brooks, (so panteth my soul after thee . . .)'

1029 Ps.119:49, 'Remember the word unto thy servant (upon which thou hast caused me to hope . . .)'

1030 'I am thy servant.'

1061 Ps.119:65, 'Thou hast dealt well with thy servant, O Lord (according unto thy word).'

1062 'And the cry comes from the heart.'

1090 Ps.119:81, 'My soul fainteth for thy salvation (but I hope in thy word . . .)'

1091 'Sweetest mother, what do you seek for your son? Wonderful!'

1114 Ps.119:97 (adapted) 'O how I love thy law, O lady . . .'

1115 'The old is passed away, everything is new.'

1143 Ps.119:113, 'I hate vain thoughts (but thy law I do love)'

1144 Ps.119:122, 'let not the proud oppress me.'

1168 Ps.119:129, 'Thy testimonies are wonderful (therefore doth my soul keep them).'

1169 Ps.144:12, '(That our sons may be) as plants grown up in their youth; (that our daughters may be as corner-stones . . .)'

1192 Ps.119:145, 'I cried with all my heart, hear me!'

1193 Ps.86:13, 'for great is thy mercy toward me.'

1215 Ps.119:161, 'Princes have persecuted me without a cause . . .'

1216-8 'All things considered, this sweetest of girls is a paradise of pleasures.'
1239 Ps.139:1, 'O Lord, thou hast searched me . . .'

'The Tunning of Elinour Rumming', p. 73
Printed fragments survive from the early 1520s; probably written c.1517. *Tunning* means 'brewing'.
1   *I chill* 'Ich will', South Eastern pronunciation.
49   i.e. she has feet like trowels.
55   i.e. with affected airs.
99   i.e. she is a fat cat.
102-3 *nappy ale* strong, sweet ale; she auctions it off as if she were selling fish at the docks.
294-300 The articles laid to pledge are weaving instruments (ll.294-5) and cloth-making instruments (ll.298-300).
297   i.e. some beggared themselves so much.
354   *Gales* Galicia, i.e. Santiago de Compostella.
381   i.e. it went down easily.
460   They were worthless because the frost had stunted their growth.
466   i.e. not worth a penny.
586-7 i.e. she pretended to be as shy as if she were waiting to dance.
610   i.e. with no money and nothing to pawn.

'Speak, Parrot', p. 91
The whole poem has to be reconstructed from two principal versions: the first half printed in *Certayne bokes compyled by mayster Skelton*, c.1545, and the second half (plus ll.1-57) found in ms. The dating of the poem as c.1521 is based on the apparent private chronology of Skelton which lies behind the numbering in the second part; 33 and 34 being the 33rd and 34th years from his first service in the royal household, in 1488. I have omitted the marginal rubrics to the poem.
28   'Who helped parrot to say Hello' (in Greek).
38   'Can speak Castilian.'
39   'Trust in yourself'; then Parrot alludes ironically to the Turkish capture of Belgrade.
40-1   'Strength without wisdom collapses on itself.'
42   'Many times . . . in memory.'

47   i.e. because of madness (*phrenesis*), understanding (*phronesis*) can not thrive.

49   'On feast days "everything" is the best.'

50   'Moderation delights.'

52   'Nothing in excess.'

55   'This hits the nail on the head.'

56   'Keep quiet . . . be silent.'

59   *Vitulus* the golden calf: the first direct reference to Wolsey, supposedly a butcher's son.

62-3 'With a mature sensibility, neither too sane nor too mad.'

69   'Shush . . . dear God of heaven, I say!'

71-7 The stanza uses Scottish ballads to warn the court about Wolsey's foreign policy.

82   *Colustrum* the finest milk.

86   *Fate* imitating the Irish pronunciation of 'water'.

91   'Every one his own way.'

95-7 'From where I produce learned arguments in the sacred school of poets.'

121-2 *Sihon . . . Og* i.e. Wolsey.

124-5 i.e. 'and asylum, once the refuge of the poor, is no longer sacred but profaned.'

133   'For the lord Judas Iscariot is great.'

141   'Only the good are beautiful,' or 'only the beautiful are good'.

151-2 i.e. they do not know how properly to construct a syllogism in Greek.

153-5 *Argolicorum* Greek; *phormio* fool; *in Capricornio* in the dark.

158   i.e. with false logic.

159   'As one of the judges.'

172-8 The established texts of grammar, law, and logic.

182   'Good morning in Greek.'

186   'With a clove.'

188   *Pleris cum musco* a sweet medicine.

193-4 'As if it were transparent, or as if it were a mirror in a riddle.'

195-7 Logical terms whose obliqueness will appeal to rhetoricians and orators, despite the logicians' scepticism about them.

199-201 'Complete confusion . . . organised confusion.'

232-3 'Parrot, behold, I sing; I know my songs are not worthy of

Phoebus, but my poetry is filled with gold.'

234-5 'According to the famous Skelton, listed in the catalogue of the Muses.'

236 1 Thess.4:18, 'Therefore console one another with these words'; following the promise of Christian immortality.

237 'Fair readers, cleverly and cunningly look after your parrot.'

269-70 'What Martial wrote will be my protection: my page is wanton, but my life is upright.'

273-4 'Life and soul'; in Latin and Greek.

275 'They lie together in Greek. This is not modest talk.'

276-9 Parrot asks the Muse to disown the vogue for spurious (and erotic) Greek verse.

285-98 These two stanzas describe Wolsey's foreign policy manoeuvrings: *Scalop* and *Cefas* are areas around Calais.

294 'Jason's golden fleece.'

306 'Let him go like an honest messenger.'

307 'The bad wish to attack the good.'

316 Punning on 'porpoise' and 'grampus'; see 'great Seal' in the next line.

330 'Parrot, go swiftly, dull the spears of fools.'

348 'Sneering behind his back.'

354 'Go speedily, Parrot, and reprove evil tongues.'

357-8 'Higher, alas, than the cedar; crueller, alas, than the leopard; alas, the ox's calf rules Priam.'

359-62 Parrot warns the king that he is ruled by a calf.

382-3 'Fly away, Parrot, moderate your muse: those who read you will scarcely understand you.'

384-5 'Parrot is known as Persius, I believe, is known; but I do not believe he (=Wolsey?) is or will be.'

386 'Cursed be the evil mouth.'

387 'My only love, the jewel of my prayers, a precious jewel is your covering.'

388-91 'Just like Aaron and the people, so the ox's calf . . .'

406 *Pinch courtesy* hold back out of politeness.

416-20 A poem in praise of Jove (=Henry VIII).

423-4 Playing on Richard Pace's messenger, used by Wolsey to solicit his papal candidature.

425 *Mala vi* with ill hail; *cy and slidder* hither and thither.

490 *Papers wearing* public humiliation for criminals.

495-501 The stanza plays on Wolsey's origins (the son of a butcher), his use of loose women (partridges and quails), and his threat to the king (the great greyhound) and the nobility (swans).

528 *Pole axes and pillars* the ornate weaponry of Wolsey's guards.

531-2 'This parrot will grow huge in my lifetime; hence my renowned Skeltonic fame will be celebrated.'

'The Garland of Laurel', p. 108

First printed 1523; its origins may well go back to 1495, with a revision in the early 1520s.

517 i.e. Chaucer, Gower, and Lydgate.

791 Silk weaving instruments: the next stanza describes the processes of weaving.

794 *Put . . . in press* began to work hard.

1167 'Mosaic gold.'

1170 The list of Skelton's works begins here. Many of them have disappeared; the survivors include 'Bouge of Court' (l.1183), 'Speak, Parrot' (l.1188), 'Magnificence' (l.1192), 'Mannerly Margery' (l.1198), 'Elinour Rumming' (l.1233), 'Colin Clout' (l.1234), and 'Philip Sparrow' (l.1255).

1310-11 Famous doctors of medicine.

1341-5 'What I have written, I have written; your wife, like a vine, you have in charge; guard her as well as you can, according to Luke, etc.' See Luke 1, the story of the birth of John the Baptist.

1353-4 'The ash on the ridge flourishes without a brook; there is none like it under the heavens without a river.'

1375 *Ragman rolls* collection of instruments by which the Scottish nobility pledged allegiance to Edward I, hence simply the meaning 'catalogue' (hence, also, 'rigmarole').

1402 *Tirikis . . . volvel* astronomical instruments.

Out of Latin into English Not strictly part of the 'Garland', these lines follow it in one edition. *To seek hallows* is to go on pilgrimage.

aforce: try
afraye: frighten
again: against
agerdouce: bitter-sweet
ale-joust: ale pot
appair: weaken
aquite: requite
array: crowd
ascry: shout
attainted: condemned

balas: a kind of ruby
balk: beam
barley-hood: drunken rage
barm: froth
baudeth: befouls
belimmed: scarred
bemole: sing B flat
bessen: dressed
beshrew: curse
bill: letter
birle: pour
ble: face
bleared thine eye: deceived you
blo: livid
blommer: uproar
bobbed: struck
bones: dice
bote: bit
bottons: buds
brake: trap
brayde, at a: suddenly
breke: breeches
bridling cast: a last throw
budget: purse

bullions: studs
bump: cry of the bittern
buss: kiss
but if: unless
byse: azure

callets: strumpets
camously: concavely
captations: attempts to get
carling: witch
case: happening
cast his craw: threw up
cawry-mawry: rough textured
chaffer: goods
chair: chariot
cheer: face
chough: jackdaw
claps: blows
clicket: vagina
clout: rag
coe: jackdaw
coistron: scullion
compass: think upon
conditions: qualities
confettered: bound
convenable: fitting
countering: improvisations
coverture: shelter
crake: crack
craze: break
creancer: tutor
crook-nebbed: hook-nosed
crowch: a coin
cuck-stool: ducking stool
culver: pigeon

curtal: a horse with a docked tail
cut, keep his: know his place

dagged: with ornamental points;
    slashed
dant: whore
daw: fool
dazing: gazing
deinte: pleasure
demean: oversee
demi: short gown
dictes: sayings
diffuse: difficult
discure: reveal
dotterel: plover; fool
douce: sweet
draff: swill
drevill: imbecile
drib: dribble
dure: last

each whit: to the full amount
ebrius: inebriated
enbullioned: studded
encheason: cause
enhatched: inlaid
ennewed: revived
enportured: ?portrayed; ?impor-
    tuned
enprowed: improved
enrailed: enclosed with
entached: studded
envive: enliven
erst: first, soonest
erst that: before

fain: sing

falyre: follower
far-fet: brought from afar
farly: wonderful
favour: countenance
feat: neat
fell: fierce
fet: fetch; well-dressed one
fizgig: gadabout
flick: flitch
float, on: full
flocket: loose, long-sleeved gar-
    ment
florth: floor
fode, play the: deceive with false
    words
fonny: foolish
fray: quarrel; fright, terror
freke: man
fret: adorned
frete: consume; chafe
frigs: rubs
frumple: tumble
fustian: pretentious
fyest: fart

gall: bitterness; sore
gambolds: leapings
gambone: gammon
gant: gannet
garded: braided, trimmed
gase: goose
gear: business
geste: tale
giggish: wanton
gill: girl
gites: skirts
glayre: adhesive

glose: deceive
go bet: get going
gore: opening in the breast of a
    gown
gowndy: bleary
gre, in: with goodwill
gressop: grasshopper
gryll: fierce
grypes: vultures

haft: seized
hallows, seek: go on pilgrimage
halsed: embraced
hardy dardy: rash daring
haskards: low fellows
haut: elevated
hayne: niggard
hent: grabbed
herber: garden
hight: is called
huckles: hips
huke: cape

ill-preving: bad luck
indifferent: neutral

jacounce: jacinth
jelofer: gillyflower
jet: fashion, strut

ken: teach
kibe: blister

lampatran: lamprey
lanner: falcon
layne: conceal
leap the hatch: run off

ledge: allege
leer: face, complexion
lefe: sweetheart
lemman: mistress
let: stop
lidderns: sluggards
links: sausages
list: wished
long: belong
lorell: rogue
losel: knave
lurdain: tramp
lure: apparatus for recalling
    hawks
lyerd: learned
lynde, light as: quick as lightning

make: mate
male: wallet
marees: marsh
martinet: martin
mavis: thrush
mawmet: idol
meed: reward
meet: fit
mell: meddle
met: measure
mewte: mew
moll: mule
morell: dark coloured horse
mowed: grimaced
mumming: performance
mur: catarrh
musket: sparrow hawk
muss: mouth

napery: linen

nebbis: nose
nept: catmint
nice: foolish
noppy: strong

ouche: brooch
ought: bore
outface: bluff
outraye: overcome

paint: pretend
pall: rich stuff
palliard: beggar
paregal: equal
pastance: pastime
paves: shield
pay: satisfaction
peke: dolt
perdurable: everlasting
pestles: legs
picking: thieving
pie: magpie
pilch: outer coat
pilling and polling: extortion
plenarly: fully
pode: toad
pole-hatchet: ?hatchet-face
popagay, popingay: parrot
porishly: with eyes half shut
port: bearing
Portingale: Portugal
pose: catarrh
postil: annotate
pounsed: perforated
Poyle: Apulia
pranked: adorned
press: crowd

prest: ready; sprightly
prick-me-dainty: fastidious
    woman
provisional: archbishop
pungete: pungent
pursuivant: suitor
puscule: pustule

quick: alive
quire: book

race: pierce
rail: shout; border
rased: slashed
ray: order, rank
ream: realm
receipt: exchequer
reconusance: acknowledgement
recueil: literary composition
rede: advice
reflare: scent
reke: consider
relucent: shining
remord: rebuke
reprobitant: condemned
resty: rancid
ribibe: old woman
road, in the: at anchor
rocket: smock coat
rood: cross
rosers: rose bushes
roufled: heaped
round: whisper
rout: mob; snore
rowth: rough
ruddes: cheeks
rued: pitied

140

ruely: sadly

sacre: a kind of falcon
sad: grave
scath: harm
scot: reckoning
scut: hare
sedean: subdean
semblant: appearance
sennight: week
shail: blunder
shap: sexual organs
shrews: rogues
shrive me: confide
shrouds: ship ropes
sib: kin
side: hanging down
sith: since
skewed: skewbald
skirgalliard: rogue
skommer: ladle
slaty: slate like
slo: slay
smaragd: emerald
snite: snipe
snur: snort
solacious: pleasurable
somedele: somewhat
sound: faint
spair: opening in a gown
sped: skilled
spence: storehouse
spick: piece of meat
spink: chaffinch
stale: decoy
start: jumped
stead: place

steep: bright
stew: brothel
stound: moment
strawry: contemptible
suffrage: prayers
supplee: pray
swinkers: labourers

tail: tally
tapettes: coverings
teen: anger
teggs: young women
threted: threatened
thurification: burning incense
tippet: scarf
tofore: before
tradition: contradiction
treat: plead
tripes: intestines
trold: spun
trow: believe
tun: barrel
tunning: brewing

unneth: scarce
utter: back

wan: dark
weasant: throat
ween: believe
weet: find out
weeting: foreknowledge
whey-wormed: pimpled
whinard: short sword
will, in: determined
wimble: gimlet
winch: kick out

wise: fashion
wist: knew
wones: lives
wood: mad
woodhack: woodpecker
worrowed: choked himself

wot, wote: know
wrench: deceit
wretchocks: puny foul
writhen: wound round

ywis: indeed